GlobalSurfNation

This is a Carlton Book

First published in 2005 by Carlton Publishing Group
20 Mortimer Street
London W1T 3JW

Copyright © Carlton Books Limited 2005

10 9 8 7 6 5 4 3 2 1

This book is sold subject to the condition that it shall not, by way of trade or otherwise, be lent, resold, hired out or otherwise circulated without the publisher's prior written consent in any form of cover or binding other than that in which it is published and without a similar condition including this condition being imposed on the subsequent purchaser. All rights reserved.

A CIP catalogue record for this book is available from the British Library

ISBN 978-1-84442-568-6

Executive Editor: Roland Hall
Project Art Direction: Darren Jordan
Designer: Ben Ruocco
Production: Lisa French

Printed and bound in Dubai

GlobalSurfNation
Surf Culture, People, History and Places

CARLTON
BOOKS

CONTENTS

Introduction	8
Hawaii	14
North America	32
Australia and New Zealand	52
Europe	72
South America	82
Africa	92
Asia and Indonesia	102

Dropping in under a feathering lip, going left and setting up for the barrel.

INTRODUCTION

Surfing is the act of standing on a board and sliding across waves. Put like that, it sounds like the easiest thing in the world to do. And in some respects it is: all you need are waves, a board and some skill – there's not much else to it. This simple and wholesome sport is loved by millions of people, but it would be fair to say that surfers rarely think about what it is that keeps them going back out for wave after wave.

Left to right: Holding the line, feeling the spray and getting spat out as the wave shuts down: pure fun.

Bent Water – if it didn't exist you'd swear it was impossible.

One thing that outsiders pick up on more readily than surfers themselves is that surfing is basically a rather strange thing to do. Indeed, it is one of the most left-field sports ever invented. Apart from the sports out there that have taken their lead from surfing – offshoots such as snowboarding and skateboarding, for example – there is little that matches the feeling of standing sideways and gliding smoothly along. Arguably, there is no other comparable activity in which people use their natural energy for competition, athletic prowess, aesthetic posing – and ultimately for fun.

It is also an ancient sport, a veritable old man compared to the rest of the popular sports on the planet. Look at its contemporaries today. Football, probably the world's most popular sport, is relatively modern; rugby didn't come to fruition until 1823; the birth of modern lawn tennis had to wait until 1873 and Formula One is obviously a latecomer to the sports arena. From what we know of surfing's complicated history, however, it has been around for well over a thousand years. And that is only a conservative estimate. We know of ancient sports – such as the running, jumping, wrestling and boxing that featured in the ancient Olympic Games – and we know of modern sports such as figure skating, hockey or badminton. Nowhere in between has there ever been anything remotely like surfing. Moreover, surfing has an aesthetic edge that aligns it more to the martial arts, or dance, than to other sports which mostly revolve around the criteria of being the fastest or the strongest. In competitions today, surfers are judged on their style, choice of wave, bravery and synchronicity with the elements. It's not simply about being first over a line, or kicking a ball in a net. In a sense, competitive surfers aren't battling against anyone else when they enter competitions: they are trying to outdo their own previous performances. Most surfers don't compete: they go surfing for surfing's sake. They just love that feeling they get from sliding across a wave – a thrilling sense of fulfilment.

Because surfing relies on mother nature to send waves, surfers must be available to go surfing at any given moment. You can't go surfing on Tuesday at 3.15 p.m. – you go surfing when there's surf. This proves problematic for a lot of people, and because the allure of the sport is so strong, many will make huge sacrifices to be able to get their fix of waves. Consequently, the sport has thrown up some interesting lifestyle choices throughout history, and the results have led surfing to where it is today in the twenty-first century.

The birth of surfing culture as we know it seems to have begun at the turn of the last century, when surfing was being resurrected from its ancient roots by a mixed group of kids living on the south shore of Oahu in the Hawaiian island chain. These young kids grew up to lead idyllic lives on Hawaii's Waikiki Beach, teaching tourists to surf, playing music on the beach, developing rescue techniques and generally starting off the whole 'beach boy' culture. From this embryonic beginning, virtually every other surfer aspired to live the same lifestyle and, with the beaches of the world virtually unpopulated, this utopian dream spread as quickly as the surf clubs could open. Soon, nearly every beach from California to Australia's Gold Coast had a lifeguard, surf scene, swimming club and all the trappings of the emerging beach culture. Of course, surfing eventually became a victim of its own success – more people wanted to live the lifestyle than the beaches and swim clubs could accommodate. When this happened, in around the 1950s, a new breed of surfer was born – one who wanted to surf when he or she wanted but wasn't about to conform to anyone's standards of how to live. They surfed, they were surfers and there wasn't much else to it.

When this breed of surfers emerged, modern surf culture was born. Typically, these people were on the periphery of society and worried more about when they could get to ride their boards than anything else. They spent their non-surfing time hanging out at the beach, spreading the belief in free thinking, art, music and the possibility of what could be done without the constraints of having a nine-to-five job. Society saw them as dropouts, stoners, lefties and conscientious objectors. The sport would almost certainly have carried on growing without them, but their added element of rock 'n' roll, rebellion and nonconformity undoubtedly added a mischievous streak that has made the sport enticing to generations since. They added a much-needed rebellious edge to surfing, one that has yet to abate.

That said, nowadays modern values are changing – people are increasingly gauging their quality of life by how much money they make or what car they drive, resulting in surfing accidentally finding itself at the forefront of discussions about modern society. Rather than merging back into the mainstream, it seems that surfing has continued on its own path and simply waited for the world to catch up. Today, with an estimated 12 million surfers worldwide, it may not be the biggest sport in the world, but it is certainly one of the most soulful.

Surfing is a sport, but it has also been called a lifestyle, a pathway and a state of mind. Perhaps this is because to go surfing one often has to travel too, and travelling has long been know to broaden horizons of every kind. When we travel we get to meet other cultures, appreciate ways of life different to our own, see with our own eyes hardships and despairs, and gain a greater understanding of the way the world works. Sometimes it's not pretty, sometimes it means we see the world at its brutal worst, but most of the time travel enables us to see the brighter side of our planet: laughter, wonders to behold and adventure to be had. Surfers tend not to see themselves as tourists but as travellers on a quest to find great waves, and because of this they often forge paths into the great unknown long before anyone has the idea of holidaying in such places. For this reason surfers have been among the first people to report back from the wilds of Africa, or remote archipelagos in the Indian Ocean; to head across islands in Indonesia, or to swim in unknown seas. Throughout the 50s and 60s, stories came back that surfers attracted crowds of indigenous peoples who watched them from the beach and marvelled at their incredible feats on the waves. Of course, on the back of such adventures and exploits whole resorts have built up, islands have become famous and the ensuring tourism has changed the face of some places altogether. That surfing has thrust western views into strange territories is unarguable; whether it has been done responsibly is debatable.

The Cutback – surfing style benchmark.

For some people in the world, the surfers who arrived at their beaches often provided the first impressions of the western world. They had never seen or met any foreigners before. Because of this, surfers had a great responsibility to get things right from the outset. Inevitably, in some places, they failed but on the whole the surf community is proud in being at the forefront of such travel adventures, nowadays dispatching envoys, boats and help to places when they're needed. Surf charities have, for example, contributed immensely towards the fight against malaria in many remote parts of Indonesia. In general, surfers like to think of themselves as people who like to do the right thing, and generally that's what they've done. Most surfers try their hardest to give back as much as they take. To be a surf traveller in the twenty-first century is to know about responsibility and how to act accordingly.

As the sport gets bigger and bigger, surfers are increasingly reflecting on what a fantastic heritage surfing has. From the Polynesian heads of state in the last millennium, through the brave riders of the 1940s, 1950s and 1960s who ultimately shaped both the sport and the lifestyle it is today, to the Olympic champions and celebrated beach boys of more recent times, today's surfers can trace their own path back to those that have been trodden before. It's our history, and we can celebrate it in unique ways. Sometimes we tend to think of past surf spots as representing a sort of surf nirvana, where waves rolled in unridden and the sun always shone. Obviously this was never the case, but as the history of the sport is constantly regurgitated, the modern surfer is inevitably reminded of what appeared to be more 'innocent' times. To start surfing now is a great thing to do, but sometimes the new surfer can feel they might have missed out on the 'golden years' of the sport. Modern riders have some incredible advantages over the surfers of yesteryear, though. In no particular order:

facilities at many beaches are superb; it's easier now to travel the world in search of waves than ever before; airlines are cheap; the infrastructures of developing countries are improving rapidly; diseases are being eradicated at many surf spots; anti-malarial pills and nets are cheap, easy to get hold of and effective; local people are aware of what the surfers have come for and are often friendly to the point of disbelief; medical facilities and insurance policies mean we're safer now in most parts of the world; we can access our money and pay for things almost anywhere in the world without the danger of carrying it all with us; we can buy boards or get repairs when we need them; we have guide books and maps, magazines, and endless years of advice to fall back on; and, of course, we can keep in contact with our friends and family when we're away too.

To some hardcore surfers these may not seem like advantages at all – for them there is still a huge, uncharted world out there – but for most surfers this is the reality of surfing today and it's not half bad.

There are several other advantages of being a surfer today, even if we don't travel. Because the sport has been through many stages of development – from huge old wooden boards to the modern thrusters ridden by surfers on the pro tour – we have a massive array of different things to ride. Learners can pick the sport up much more quickly if they start on big, foam boards and then work their way down in size; good surfers can pick locally shaped boards from most good surf breaks that will work specifically for the type of conditions they're likely to encounter. Today's board makers know almost everything there is to know about board construction. They know what fins work, what thickness of board works, how much bend the board should have, how it should be finished, what shape it should be, how long it should be and so on. This information is the result of millions of hours of trial and error, and the modern surfer can simply walk into a shop and gain access to it by buying a modern board.

One crucial difference between surfing and any other modern sport is that surfers can pick a type of surfing and get the equipment to do that job. For example, if we liked the way Gerry Lopez surfed in the 1970s we can get a board that is an exact replica of the one

he surfed. We can now longboard like they did in San Onofre in the 50s, try out 80s twin-finned boards, have a beautiful balsa wood board, get the latest high-performance thruster, try a massive big-wave 'gun' or, if we're really good, have a tow-in board made and try our luck out in some enormous waves. For our forefathers, such a broad range of equipment designs and retro styles wasn't possible. They may have had emptier waves, but we can do more on our waves today.

Surf history, therefore, is a double-edged sword. We shouldn't get too carried away with the notion that there's nothing left to explore, no new waves to ride or anything left that hasn't been done before. Nor should we be complacent about what surfing pioneers have done for us. But we must find a balance between their views and how we will have to all get along as the world gets smaller and there are less waves for everyone. The realization that there is a huge value in the history of surfing has led to reflections on every facet of the sport: the art, the board shapes, the heroes and villains, the films and magazines and the music – all slotted nicely into the third millennium of the sport's existence. Today we can look back at almost any part of surfing's past and appreciate what part it had to play in today's sport. We now have surf historians, surf artists, surf films and surf music. The Beach Boys, Dick Dale and other groups of the 50s and early 60s made the initial inroads into that genre, but today, in Jack Johnson, Donovan Frankenreiter and Scott Sullivan among others, we have some genuine surf musicians, playing to packed audiences of surfers and non-surfers around the world.

Everywhere we look, surfing seems to be intertwined with something or someone. To be a surfer today is to be part of a massive subculture that has a voice, is proud of its roots and has a good idea of the path it is taking for the future.

Perhaps the greatest thing about surfing is the ease with which new members are affiliated to this cross-continental sport – there is no membership card to fill out, there are no fees to pay – and contrary to the fashion pages of some magazines, you don't even have to wear a uniform. No, all you have to do to become a surfer today is to love sliding along waves. It's the absolute bottom line for every surfer out there.

Lines of swell wrap around a Polynesian reef and form a perfect left hand break.

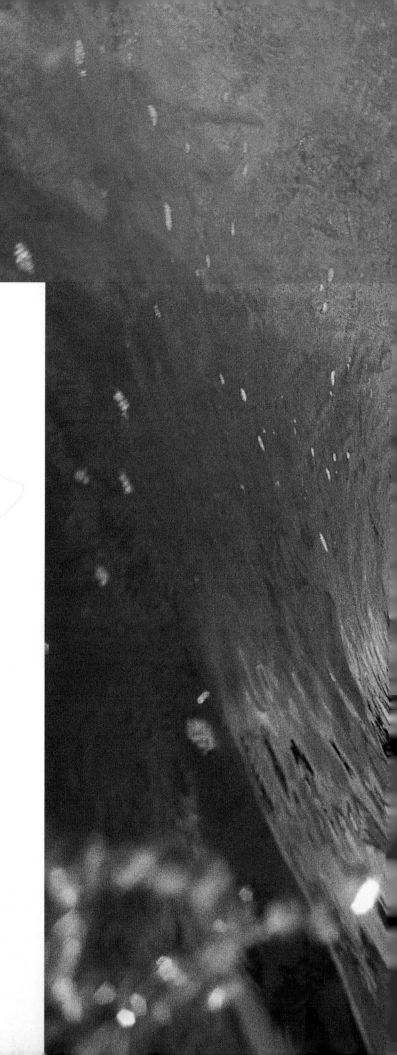

HAWAII

Hawaiian walls have always tested surfers.

History

Hawaii comprises over one hundred islands, but we think of the main chain as being the islands of Maui, Hawaii (called The Big Island by locals to avoid confusion), Lanai, Molokai, Kauai and Oahu, which houses the capital Honolulu. For 60 million years after they erupted as volcano peaks from the Pacific, the islands were essentially barren, haphazardly inheriting wind-blown seeds, large winged birds and various plants, as and when they arrived. We often think of them as idyllic places, an earthly paradise perhaps, but in fact it's more likely they were evolutionary anomalies, and certainly no land mammals arrived on the islands until around AD 300, when the first wave of humans voyagers colonized them as part of one of the greatest yet least-known acts of exploration – the Polynesian Voyages. These first visitors were no accidental travellers – we know they brought families, as well as domesticated animals such as pigs, dogs and enough plants with them to start colonies. More importantly for us, a second wave of Polynesian explorers arrived around AD 900. And these people did something no one else on the planet did: they surfed.

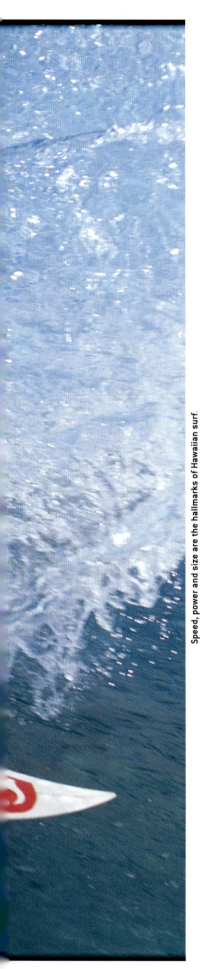

Speed, power and size are the hallmarks of Hawaiian surf.

Aloha – Welcome.

We know from the legends and oral histories of the islands that surfing was ingrained into the islanders' ancient culture at a deep level. One could be killed for surfing on the wrong wave, gamble one's life in a surfing contest, take sexual favours for someone sharing a wave, or woo a wife or husband with one's skill. Mo'iheki, a celebrated chief who lived around the 10th Century, is famous for taking two sisters as his wives after impressing them with his surfing prowess somewhere on the island of Kauai. Although little of this original surf culture survives, we can safely assume that they surfed for the same reason we do now: because it's fun.

We also know that the sport became a national pastime, and was enjoyed by men and women of all ages and status. We even know that some spots were so good for surfing that the ruling classes deemed them fit only for chiefs, forbidding any commoners to ride there. Clearly, surfing was important for the Hawaiians, and the kudos that came from being a good surfer can easily be imagined in a society that depended on the sea for its survival.

North Shore energy being released in the tradtional way.

No wonder this is a surfer's paradise.

For much of Polynesia (the general term for all the islands in the Pacific), all this changed with the arrival of Europeans in the 16th Century. Although Hawaii had probably been visited by several ships before this time, it was a latecomer to the party and only officially became known to the western world when Captain James Cook arrived there in 1778. The island's size, geographical position and ability to provision sea-worn ships meant that international trading nations coveted the islands. Treaties were signed, ports sprang up and on paper everything was above board and legitimate. But if it was a boon for the European ships and traders, Hawaii's discovery was a death knell for the traditional Hawaiian way of life. Soon after Cook's arrival, disease spread through the islands, followed in 1820 by a wave of religious cleansing. If those two thunderbolts hadn't taken enough of a toll on this fragile and ancient culture, the final blow came when commercial exploitation entered the equation. People didn't have time to surf and were discouraged from doing so; in fact, they were simply struggling to survive. By the late 19th Century these powerful forces had stripped away much of Hawaii's ancestry, replacing it with a western government, western beliefs and a code of morals that was determined by a religion rooted on the other side of the world.

By the turn of the century, while Europe was dividing up the world into empires and building up to the First World War, surfing — the last bastion of Polynesian cultural heritage — was hanging by a thread. Already a thing of the past on most islands in the Pacific, the simple act of surfing on water survived by the skin of its teeth on the island of Oahu, thanks to small pockets of people who clearly just couldn't give it up. Without them, you wouldn't be reading this book.

But survive it did, eventually being resurrected by the unlikely combination of immigrant kids and the children of some local families living around Honolulu on the island of Oahu. One of them, Duke Kahanamoku, went on to become a two-time Olympic medallist and the universally acclaimed father of modern surfing. His achievements deserve a book on their own (in fact, he has already been the subject of two biographies) as do the exploits of other early surfers such as the Hawaiian-Irish immigrant son George Freeth who had to learn most of his skills from scratch. Those pioneers knew that the boards were used to stand on, and they knew they had to 'catch' a wave, but apart from those basics, everything about the sport had to be learnt again.

Within a few years however, these kids were starting to get the hang of it. Freeth was even stand-up riding. All the sport needed now was a bit more of a publicity push to get it back on track.

Enter Jack London, one of the most famous authors of his generation. London arrived in Waikiki Beach in 1907 having been commissioned to wire back his travel exploits to various magazines and papers; his notes would also form the basis for a book. While in Hawaii he was introduced to Freeth and went out to tackle surfing. Famed for his adventure writing, and already a proven man of action, London fell in love with the sport. His landmark article 'Riding the South Seas Surf' – which oddly enough first saw light of day in a magazine entitled *A Woman's Home Companion* – was churned out while London was still sunburnt from a surfing session he'd enjoyed. For the readers back on the mainland it was literary gold, and from that time on it would have been hard to keep the sport under wraps.

Surfing was back on its feet and in London had a patron who was willing to back it. But surfing's renaissance didn't stop with London's piece. In the 1912 Olympics, virtual unknown Duke Kahanamoku won a swimming gold medal in spectacular and convincing style. And he put his success down to surfing. The world's press couldn't get enough of this news. Here was a tall, proud, Hawaiian man who embodied the spirit of surfing and the gentleness of the Polynesian race. Surfing couldn't have wished for a better figurehead to come along at a better point in history. That Duke dedicated his life to spreading the love of surfing is well known. His fame helped kick off a micro-surf industry around Waikiki, where tourists could come and try out this sport, hang with the other 'beach boys' as they were called, and maybe meet the great man himself. Duke died penniless, though much-loved, yet it could be said that his actions laid down the blueprint for modern surfers: he competed only against himself, challenged but respected the ocean and throughout his life advocated the belief that surfing was Hawaii's gift to the world. Today there's a statue of him on Waikiki Beach and every day of the year it is drenched in flowers.

From the 1920s onwards, surfing's popularity continued to grow throughout the islands – and subsequently, the world. Although boards, attitudes and numbers have changed, little else has altered since Duke and his contemporary beach boys. They surfed for the same reasons as you or I, and they did it with similar actions, on similar waves and using similar equipment. Today, surfing has reached every corner of the globe, yet Hawaii – the place that undoubtedly nurtured the sport, if not invented it – is still hailed as the best place in the world to do it. There just seems to be something in the water there.

Surf Spot: Waimea

That Hawaii is synonymous with surfing goes without saying, and while it played a crucial part in the sport's history, the surfers who live there spend little time reflecting on their heritage from day to day. Instead, they continue to surf all year round, trying to push the boundaries of the sport ever further forward and riding bigger and heavier waves. Today's challenge of taking on the most dangerous waves in the islands is mounted using jet skis, buoyancy vests and boards with foot straps. While this is a sport for professionals and serious surfers only, the islands still hold enough kudos to attract visiting riders, keen to make the pilgrimage to the world's surfing mecca – the North Shore of Oahu.

On this seven-mile stretch of beach, also known as Pau Malu in the local language, lie some of the most consistent, awe-inspiring waves ever created by mother nature. At the north end, the breaks of Velzyland, Sunset, Rocky Point and Backyards dominate; at the south, the rides of Avalanche and Himalayas are there to be buried under. In the middle of all this sit two of the most famous waves to ever roll into shore: the Banzia Pipeline and Waimea Bay.

Although Pipeline, as it's often called, is probably the most photographed wave in the world, it's Waimea Bay that seems to be the ultimate wave among surfers. But that hasn't always been the case. After a sharp rise from deep sea, a reef outside the bay picks up the giant swells that pump into the island and forms an enormous wave that breaks within touching distance of some huge rocks and peels right towards the middle of the bay. An ancient temple (or 'Heiau', to give it its Polynesian title) overlooks the break, and a modern church dominates the skyline. Rock carvings nearby suggest ancient Polynesian riders may well have taken the waves on here, but there is no reliable record of the event. After the death of Dickie Cross, a surfer who died in 1943 simply trying to paddle back to shore after the waves got too big, Waimea Bay was generally considered off limits and un-rideable to the surfers of the 30s, 40s and 50s. The idea of riding a wave here was considered more than stupid: it was tantamount to suicide.

That all changed, however, when a group of surfers paddled out on November 7, 1957. In the same year that Russia launched the first animal into space, Greg Noll – along with Mike Stange, Mickey Munoz, Pat Curren, Bing Copeland, Del Cannon and Bob Bernell – entered the realm of big-wave riding. "It was simple," said Noll after they had all returned safely to shore. "The ocean didn't swallow us up and the world didn't stop turning."

For the next 25 years, Waimea remained the pinnacle of surfing, the ultimate test of courage and skill. Today, its claws have been dulled by the exploits of the Billabong Odyssey and the K2 Challenge – both ongoing annual prizes for the world's biggest wave, that regularly include those found in the middle of the ocean or in far-flung destinations – but Waimea is still one of the most feared and respected and best-loved waves among the surfing community. It is also home to the Quiksilver contest, held in memory of Eddie Aikau, which is often referred to as The Eddie. The contest, which benefits from the natural amphitheatre of the bay itself, features the world's best surfers paying their respects to Aikau, who died in 1978 on the Polynesian Voyaging Canoe Hokule'a. It is perhaps the most authentic gladiatorial spectacle that is hosted in the 21st Century. Whenever waves are predicted to be over 20ft (6m) high within the contest period, which runs from December to February, the whole island of Oahu wakes up early in the hope it will be on. When it is, Waimea is once again the most talked about and respected wave in the world.

Huge waves push towards the islands like freight trains. To ride them is to confront fear.

HAWAII. 23.

Profile: Gerry Lopez

The name Gerry Lopez is one that even non-surfers will recognize, yet with his slight, athletic build, he hardly epitomises the image of the heavily muscled big-wave surfer. At 5'8" (1.73m) and a mere 135lb (61kg), you'd be forgiven for thinking that he wouldn't last long in the kind of crushing, heavy surf that has claimed the lives of many a stronger, more robustly built surfer. However, there is perhaps no surfer who more clearly defines the art of tube riding, and Gerry — with his catlike grace, uncanny sense of timing and incredible poise under pressure — has become an icon in surfing culture. In the words of fellow surf legend Tom Curren, "Gerry was made for the barrel."

After four decades of board riding, Gerry Lopez is still hooked on the ride.

Born in Hawaii in 1948, Gerry Lopez first learned to surf in the mellow breakers of Waikiki, near his home in Honolulu. The construction of a harbour channel and breakwater at the Ala Moana reef created near-perfect surfing conditions there, and Gerry began to fine-tune his skills. It was here that he first caught sight of a surfer getting barrelled – though it was such a new thing that, at the time, no one knew what to call it. After spending a year at college in California (where, with typical humility, he describes how he got on a local surf-shop team by "being from Hawaii and knowing how to surf a little"), he became properly embroiled in the late 60s' surf frenzy, moving back to Hawaii with the sole aim of spending as much time as possible in the water. By the winter of 1968–69 he had graduated to the imposing waves of the North Shore and was beginning to generate quite a media buzz, making his first appearance in Surfer magazine and establishing himself as the dominant surfer at Pipeline. Although the nickname 'Mr Pipeline' had been given to a couple of worthy surfers before him, it soon passed on to Gerry and there it stayed.

Throughout the 1970s, Gerry could be seen dropping into and charging gracefully through barrel after barrel on boards with their own distinctive logo. That logo, a lightning bolt striking the middle of the board, was his own venture, a company that he set up with his friend Jack Shipley in 1971 at the height of his fame. Gerry had been shaping boards for some time, an interest of his that went right back to his first ever surfboard, which had a smashed-up nose and was bought second-hand for him by his dad: "It not only launched me on my surfing career but also, in repairing the nose, it launched what was to become the vocation which was instrumental in allowing me to pursue the career in surfing," he comments. This is something that Gerry has evolved alongside his surfing, and he was instrumental in the development of the first tow-in boards in the early 90s, which allowed surfers to ride the monstrous outer reef waves such as Jaws for the first time. Gerry then moved from shaping the boards to joining the tow-in movement for himself, riding some of the heaviest and most intimidating waves on the planet.

Although Lightning Bolt had become the surf industry success of the 1970s, by the early 80s the company had fallen apart due to internal power struggles – a most inopportune time for this to happen, as the surf-wear boom had begun in earnest and relative newcomers with little surfing pedigree were making huge amounts of money. Lopez, however, had sold his interest in 1980, some time before the crunch, using the money to build a house on the beach at Pipeline. Each of the five bedrooms had a view of the surf break. At this backyard surf spot he enjoyed the next ten years, travelling to Indonesia to surf at a new spot that had been discovered in the southeastern end of Java named G-Land, learning to windsurf and eventually meeting the woman who was to become his wife – Toni.

His numerous appearances on the big screen have helped to make Gerry Lopez one of the more recognisable faces of surfing. Things took off after he was asked to play himself in John Milius's *Big Wednesday*, and he was subsequently offered the role of Arnold Schwarzenegger's sidekick Subotai in *Conan the Barbarian*. Next followed another appearance as himself in *North Shore* in 1987, then a role as a Dayak in *Farewell to the King* in 1990, which starred Nick Nolte. Milius was greatly impressed by Lopez's ability to pick up new skills: "He learns so fast. In Conan, Gerry was the first to learn the swordsmanship; then he taught Arnold and the others. He's amazing, really. He can run 40 miles, swim wherever he has to, and I don't think even he knew how good he was on a motorcycle." Clearly, Gerry just likes doing movies. Acting has simply become another string to the Lopez bow.

These days, Gerry lives with his wife Toni and son, Alex, two hundred miles inland in the mountains of Bend, Oregon. Here he can easily indulge in his new passion: snowboarding, something Toni introduced him to in the winter of 1990–91 during a Christmas spent with her family in the mountains of southern California. "She rented some snowboard equipment and took me to the snow for the first time," he recounts. "Our very first run down the hill on snowboards had us excited as kids about this new sport and we both knew we had to have more of it." After spending a few weeks taking lessons in Aspen, Colorado, he was hooked. "That was that. My snowboarding career was launched."

Now that he spends more time snowboarding, Gerry's surfing is kept up to scratch by riding a standing wave in a nearby irrigation ditch. However, he points out that this is by no means the end of the story. "For the time being, I snowboard more than I surf, but I will never stop being a surfer at heart, I really have no choice. Waves on the ocean, snow on the mountain, riding them both in the same way is a total meditative physical mantra that can open the doors of your inner self, the place where all the mystical potentialities of the universe are realized. I get to the beach whenever I can and in a way, I get more than ever from the surf when I'm there, maybe because I don't have it all the time like I used to. At some point we will return to the seaside and I will take up where I left off; meanwhile I just get it where I can."

A long believer in yoga, Gerry practices what he preaches on an Indonesian boat trip.

Profile: Keala Kennelly

On the girls' world surfing tour Keala Kennelly stands out from the pack. Most people in the know consider that she is in line to win the World Championship almost as a matter of course, and regard her surfing style, power and go-for-it attitude as being almost unequalled within women's surfing. Out of the ocean, Keala is also the most rebellious rock 'n' roll surf star on the tour, regularly going in her own direction and not caring about the consequences. This combination of talent and strong character sometimes rubs the established surf industry up the wrong way. Which is exactly how it should be, isn't it?

Perhaps Keala's forthright attitude comes from her unconventional upbringing. Born on the island of Kauai in the Hawaiian chain, she grew up within what would be considered a hippy environment, living in a geodesic dome and being fairly embarrassed at the lack of money and the free-spirited conduct of her parents. Because of the underlying racial tension in Hawaii, and because of her blonde hair and white skin, Keala wasn't readily accepted by the locals, especially at Kapaa High School on the island's East Side, where she quickly learned to fight to survive. She discovered that surfing was the perfect way for her to let out any aggression she might have harboured and, fortunately, she met two other kids in a similar predicament who made the same step with her — brothers Andy and Bruce Irons.

The social injustices that beset Hawaii and its indigenous people are well documented. The cataclysmic events of the last 250 years of European meddling have resulted in a feeling among most Polynesian descendents that they've been cheated out of their islands. The fact that they tend to be in a minority, have the lowest average incomes and are constantly being outpriced as house prices soar, only fuels the fire. It's often said that it's the children who pay for their parents' mistakes, and certainly every generation of kids who are born in today's Hawaii inherits this terrible legacy. Surfing is a great leveller, though, and for many kids it is a natural way of leaving those problems on the beach, and forging self-made reputations in the waves. To be a good surfer in Hawaii is to earn acceptance and to claw back some credit from the unjust deficit you were born with — no matter what race you are.

Very early on, Keala showed that she had enormous natural energy, surfing so much and with such skill that she was taking on the boys and beating them at their own game. This 110 per cent commitment spilled over into everyday life too. On dry land she made a disastrous move to California with a 'psycho' boyfriend at 16, rebelled against her parents and did all the things troubled teens do. Keala did them with the pace of a Tasmanian Devil. But they say what doesn't kill you makes you stronger and Keala picked herself up, surfed even harder than before and focused on what she needed to do.

"My favourite type of waves are big heaving barrelling lefts like Teahupoo and Pipeline," she said in a recent interview. It's no coincidence they are also considered the two most deadly waves in the world by virtually every surfer in existence.

Perhaps it helped her that the two kids she grew up with, Andy and Bruce, have also gone on to be ranked at the top of the world leader board, but there's no mistaking that it is Keala's own natural confidence that has pushed her to become such a great surfer as well as a great competitor too. The inner fire that has always driven her on takes her surfing to new levels. The 2003 and 2004 World Championship leader boards make it obvious that she's locked in a fierce battle against Australia's Layne Beachley. "Keala is always the one to beat," said Beachley during her 2003 World Championship campaign. Clearly, it didn't sit well with Kennelly to be in second place. After several years working up the rungs, she now wants to take her rightful place at the top. At a recent Triple Crown Series in Hawaii – considered by many to be the ultimate Hawaiian accolade – she showed her true feelings in an interview with the Hawaiian Star Bulletin: "My main focus is the [world] title. If I win the Triple Crown along with the title, that would be great."

Keala takes on another Tahitian monster at Teahupo.

The win will surely come, and when it does it will surely be a release for Keala. Marketing men for the big surf companies are scouring the globe in search of great-looking women who can ride a wave, but Keala has always remained focused on what really matters: her surfing prowess. Somewhat spurned by the surf industry because of her reputation for being a tough cookie, Keala has developed her own style – partying hard, DJing on the tour, hanging out with her Pussy Posse and doing what she wants when she wants it "I just can't sit, gotta dance all night," she said at a recent North Shore party. "So what?"

People have told her to calm down but she shows no sign of doing that. A world title would be the biggest middle finger to her critics, and it's perhaps this motivation that is pushing her so hard. A win will not only make her name in the record books, but put her in the same vein as the John McEnroes of this world. Maybe this is exactly what surfing needs right now. Time will tell.

Away from the surfing industry, Keala is a different person altogether. "I try to treat others the way I would like to be treated," she said recently, "because I think that is a great way to live. And if I see somebody without a smile, I try to give them one of mine."

Local Brands

Dakine
Established: In 1979 by Rob Kaplan, who started making surf leashes from his home on Maui.
www.dakine.com

Hawaiian Island Creations
Established: In 1971 by Honoluluan brothers Stephen and Jimmy Tsukayama. Now makes everything from T-shirts to boards with a worldwide chain of shops.
www.hicsurf.com

Da Hui
Established: In 1975 by Kawiki Stant Senior and Brian Amona on Oahu's infamous North Shore. Da Hui is the only Polynesian ancestry surf brand and they are very proud of their roots.
www.dahui.com

Town and Country
Established: In 1971 by Craig Sugihara out of Pearl Harbor City and now an international surf brand.
www.tcsurf.com

Local Shaper

Dick Brewer
Established: Founded Surfboards Hawaii in 1961 and has since gone on to shape for every major surfer of the last four decades. Probably the most famous shaper around.
Kind of boards he makes: Every shape, but most famous these days for big-wave guns and tow-in short boards.
www.plumeriasurfboards.com

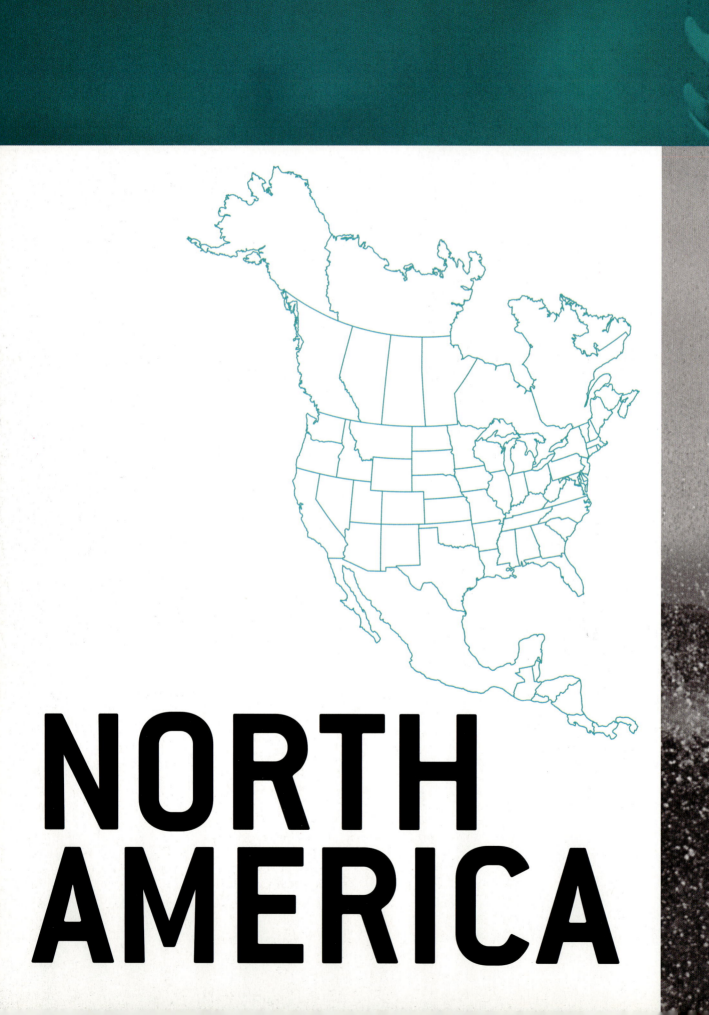

NORTH AMERICA

Aerials – skate and snowboard-influenced surfing.

History

The USA in general, and California in particular, has been synonymous with surfing ever since it embraced the sport early in the 20th Century. Like Hawaii, the climate, swell and beach culture of the West Coast combine to make it ideal for nurturing such a sport. For want of a better expression, it is a surfer's paradise. Unlike Hawaii, however, its surfing history is traceable to fairly recent events.

In all probability, the first people to ride surfboards off mainland North America were three Hawaiian princes – Jonah Kuhio Kalanianaole, David Kawananakoa and Edward Keliiahonui – who surfed at Santa Cruz in front of astonished crowds when they were enlisted at a military school near San Francisco. They even made the news in the *Santa Cruz Daily* in 1885 under the headline 'Beach Breezes'. However, although they were certainly torchbearers of the sport, this very early attempt at introducing surfing into the continent fizzled out almost as soon as they left the beach. It was a stillborn attempt to get the sport off the ground.

Whether other attempts at introducing surfing were made around this time will doubtless emerge in due course, but modern surf historians tend to agree that when George Freeth sailed from Hawaii in July of 1907, he did so with the express purpose of introducing the sport to mainland America and is therefore credited as being the godfather of North America's surfing heritage. He even carried papers by the Hawaiian Promotion Committee – which had been recently set up to promote the Hawaiian lifestyle and tourist industry. Moreover, his timely arrival was well publicized, since he was the featured star in Jack London's groundbreaking article 'Riding the South Seas Surf', which set the imagination of would-be surfers alight the same year.

Steadily, after numerous surfing demonstrations by Freeth to huge crowds up and down the West Coast, Californians began to see the sport as a healthy addition to their sun-drenched lives. Once the word was out, surfing spread quickly. From Santa Cruz all the way down to the Mexican border, endless breaks were discovered, ridden and enjoyed. Freeth helped enormously, advocating life-saving and winning congressional medals for his brave rescues and pioneering water-safety techniques. Sadly he died from Spanish Influenza in 1919 at the age of only 35, but by then his mission to get people in the water was complete, with regular surf haunts now established along most of the coast.

Without doubt, the centres of surfing during the 1930s were the breaks of Palos Verdes, Long Beach and San Onofre. While they still held some of the values of the Hawaiian sport – most surfers belonged to a surf or swimming club and aspired to be lifeguards rather than simply surfers – their proximity to ship builders, the wood trade and a certain 'Wild West' spirit enabled them to start messing around with their equipment in ways that Hawaiians would have regarded as disrespectful. Tom Blake is credited with adding a fin to his surfboard in 1934; hollow boards started to appear; lighter materials and shorter lengths were in use; and generally speaking the sport took on a wholly Californian feel. The future looked bright.

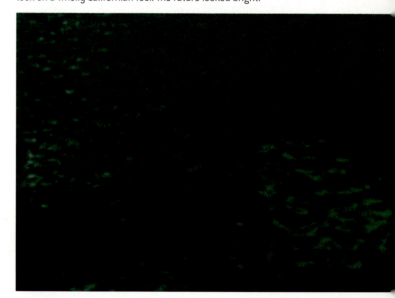

Barrel riding will always be the ultimate surfing goal.

In all probability, surfing would have gone from strength to strength, gaining popularity and wide acceptance as a healthy pursuit for young men and women. After all, most of the professional swimmers of the time had started as surfers, and they were going on to become Olympic champions – and even Hollywood stars (Buster Crabbe, Johnny Weissmuller and Duke Kahanamoku all made the transition from the sea to the silver screen). But World War Two arrived for America in 1941, sweeping through the surfing demographic with little regard for the wishes of the generation.

When beach culture returned after the war, there was a noticeable shift in attitude. A generation that had given up valuable years of their lives to fight, often losing friends in the process, came home feeling disillusioned and cheated. The military swallowed up vast tracks of coastal land, closing down many surf spots in the process. The days of communal, jovial surf meets and swimming clubs were numbered – surfers had developed an attitude and while it wasn't wholly anti-authoritarian, it certainly bordered on what we could consider to be confrontational. The teens coming up through the beach ranks didn't want to become lifeguards; they just wanted to surf.

However, the war did bring in welcome technological changes to boards. Fibreglass had been invented during the conflict; engineers who had access to studies of ships' hulls were able to make improvements to the boards, while increased knowledge of materials enabled board prices to come down. During the late 1940s, ships heading to Hawaii increasingly carried more and more surfers eager to head out and ride the breaks at Waikiki, Makaha and the newly rediscovered North Shore or Pau Malu Beach. When the Hawaiian and US surf cultures met, mixed and dispersed, they created a scene that rapidly became self-supporting. What we now consider the global surf industry was being born.

Staying with the curl will always pay dividends.

Back in California, Malibu was rapidly becoming the epicentre for a new surf attitude. By the late 1950s, the riders were starting to hate what they considered to be 'wannabe' surfers. To get away from the crowded waves they started going on exploratory surf trips to Mexico, Baja and – of course – Hawaii. These were what surf historians tend to think of as the 'golden years' of surfing. But in reality it was a fragile era for the sport. The Gidget phenomenon (more of which anon) exploded in 1959, as a direct result of the Malibu scene, but the tiny, fragmented and self-contained surf industry wasn't in any way prepared for the bombardment of outsiders trying to grab a piece of this happening sport. Hollywood wanted to film it, magazines wanted to feature it, book publishers wanted to fictionalize it, and anyone with a factory wanted to mass-produce some sort of surfing innovation. Throughout the late 1950s and early 1960s the sport had a strange half-and-half existence. On the one hand, surfers such as Miki Dora, Micky Munoz and Greg Noll were happily standing in for actors in films such as *Ride The Wild Surf* (1964); on the other, surfers who had ridden for years were bemoaning the fact that their precious sport was slipping away from them as an ever-increasing influx of new riders made the waves crowded and less fun to surf. Surfing was getting popular, and the popular riders were promoting it, yet everyone was becoming frustrated by the amount of interest their actions were generating. The effect of mass exposure was seemingly lost on those young surfers who were dabbling with the professional aspects of the sport.

Cutting back to stay with the wave.

However, by the end of the 60s there was no going back. Surfing as a sport was open to the masses, and they loved it. Although it had taken over a thousand years, this 'Sport of Kings', as Jack London had dubbed it, was spearheading a global counterculture revolution. Whereas once it had been about hula, ukulele and races to the beach, it was now about slashing and destroying the wave, surf guitar licks, attitude and rebelling. Drugs, partying and rock 'n' roll entered the equation, helping to distance the sport from the more traditional realms of team pursuits such as football and baseball. Of course, you didn't have to be at the far extreme of society to go surfing, but to many surfing was becoming a lifestyle, a welcome outlet for energy, and a release for a huge cross-section of people and cultures. It also started to spawn offshoots, such as skateboarding, sidewalk surfing, skim boarding and – eventually – snowboarding, hand-in-hand with an ever more underground, rebellious 'punk' attitude.

The modern culture of board-riding was up and running and California was its proving ground.

NORTH AMERICA. 38

Surf Spot: Malibu

From Santa Cruz's Steamer Lane and the dangerous big wave of Mavericks down to San Diego's La Jolla Cove, California is a veritable smorgasbord of different waves and self-styled 'Surf Cities'. And why not? With over a thousand miles of coastline, all looking out into the vast Pacific Ocean, it is perfectly placed to absorb some of the most consistent swell in the world.

And while there are literally waves on every beach, perhaps the most famous break in California is the fantastic right-hand point break of Malibu, just north of present-day Los Angeles. At the banquet of surf exploration, Malibu was a relative latecomer to the table. That it took so long to find this world-class wave is understandable when you consider that for 20 years after surfing's arrival in the state, the wave broke in the middle of a huge area of privately owned coastline. Violently opposing California's growth, the owners even employed armed security to keep trespassers out. Thus, Malibu remained unsurfed even as the sport flourished across the rest of the state.

However, when a compulsory purchase order opened up the land to build what is now the Pacific Highway along the coast, Malibu's riches were laid bare for all to see and, unsurprisingly, it didn't take long before it was ridden. While the highway was still under construction, legendary pioneering surfers Tom Blake and Sam Reid snuck in on September 1926 to became the first surfers to ride this heavenly wave. Gliding their solid, ten-foot redwood boards across perfect three-foot waves clearly made an impression: within a few months the word was out and surfers from nearby breaks came to see what all the fuss was about.

Some lip tricks are borrowed directly from skateboarding.

The wave itself hasn't ever really been considered a dangerous or challenging break – its peeling rights and sheer lengths of rides are the main attractions – but shortly after the Second World War, Malibu garnered a reputation as a place to be reckoned with. Rather than fear the wave itself, people began to fear the surfers who rode it. During the 50s, surfers came to hang out, ride, play music, form gangs, invent and modify their equipment (the Malibu surfboard came to fruition there) and taunt surfers from other breaks. Riders such as Miki Dora, Bob Simmons and Terry 'Tubesteak' Tracy garnered reputations for being tough surfers who guarded their break like jealous boyfriends. Outsiders were definitely not welcome. Unsurprisingly, this birth of 'localism' was perversely attractive to younger potential surfers, who looked up to this gang of surf rebels with attitude.

While rock 'n' roll was defining a generation on the radio, surfing was finding its feet on Malibu Beach. The surfers were rebelling against army conscription, consumerism and McCarthy-era America. Clearly there was something attractive about this rebellion – future Hollywood stars such as Norma Jean Baker came to hang out with the surfers, Malibu became popular and apparently lots of people saw something

The curtain is about to fall on this performance.

appealing about the Malibu gangs and their bad-boy image. It even became popular to rubbish other local breaks and nearby surfers.

Ironically, this insular and suspicious group exploded on to an international stage after a girl named Kathy Kohner attempted to surf at Malibu. According to legend, Tubesteak said she looked like a girl midget and nicknamed her 'Gidget'. The tale of her life – including the way she managed to gain acceptance into this crowd, the partying and the thrill of this new beach lifestyle – became world famous when her father wrote a semi-fictional book entitled *Gidget* and sold the film rights to the story. When the first Gidget film came out in 1959, Malibu's popularity soared, adding even greater numbers to the already overcrowded wave and leaving it in much the same situation as it is in now. When it works it is still magical, but the chances of riding in alone and in the same conditions as when Blake and Reid first surfed are virtually nil.

The view into the barrel.

Surf Spot: The Space Coast

Florida lies at the southeast corner of North America, a location that blesses the state with a generously warm, Caribbean climate. However, due to its position in relation to the vast continental mass to the west, it suffers from horrendous weather during the hurricane season from July through to October. Ironically, it's this danger that produces the best swells to hit the Atlantic coast of the state, and from the summer onward, Florida can be hit by huge swells, or lull in relatively flat swells, depending on what storms are active in the ocean. Add in the fact that the state is also home to alligators, and is bordered by the world's most notorious ocean in terms of shark attacks, and it's a wonder why anyone would ever get in the water at all.

Catching air.

Slashing a wave results in huge spray coming off the board.

And yet like Californians, Floridians have made surfing their favourite pastime. Of the thousand miles of rideable coastline, perhaps the most famous surf area is the Space Coast, situated around the city of Melbourne, roughly halfway along the Atlantic edge of the state. Sebastian Inlet is probably the most famous break in the area, where three peaks pose some challenging riding, from a solid tubing left-hander to a backwashing-wedgy peak, which is perfect to launch airs off. Further north along the coast is Melbourne City's beach, where the Indialantic Boardwalk provides makeable barrels for good surfers, and is home to Florida's big-wave venue RC's. To drive between breaks any surfer has to drive along the fantastic A1A, which runs parallel to the coast and provides unrestricted views to any passing wave. If there was ever such a thing as a surf highway, it would be this main thoroughfare along Florida's east side.

While these beaches are good news for locals and travellers alike, it is inarguably Cocoa Beach that draws in the tourists. Why? Well, put simply it is an average beach-break that has the glorious claim to fame of being right next door to the Cape Canaveral Kennedy Space Center, home of the space shuttle and the site of the launches. Surfers and beach-goers alike come to look out for jets streaming into the air force base that sits alongside the Space Center. And many of those surfers probably sit out at the back of the waves and dream of becoming the next Kelly Slater, who grew up surfing on this very same stretch of beach.

Profile: Lisa Andersen

Maybe they put something in the water in Florida. After all, the state has produced two of the best and most competitively successful surfers in the world: Kelly Slater, and female surfing sensation Lisa Andersen.

The tale of Andersen's rise to her position as the dominant female surfer of the 1990s is an unlikely one. Born in Long Island in 1969, she spent much of her early life in the hills of Fork Union, Virginia. The daughter of a Danish father and a New York-born mother, it wasn't until 1983, when her family moved to Ormond Beach, Florida, that she ever tried surfing. The 14-year-old Lisa took to the sport instantly, and it wasn't long before her interest developed into a full-blown obsession. Unfortunately, this was something that her parents chose to discourage, thinking that it exposed her to the worst sort of bums and dropouts, and they used whatever means they could to discourage her passion. Such was their concern over their daughter's determination to hang out with people they considered 'druggies' that her mother even forced her to take a drug test — at least in part due to her worry that Lisa would take after her father, a heavy drinker who used physical punishment to discipline his errant daughter. She was threatened with house arrest, and attendance at a strict evening mealtime was enforced after which Lisa wasn't allowed out. On one occasion her father stepped on her board, breaking its fins.

Despite the acute displeasure of her family, Lisa never faltered in her determination to follow her chosen path, and surfing continued to hold her firmly in its thrall. In June 1985, as soon as she was out of school, she upped sticks and

Lisa Andersen on her way to another world title.

moved out west, famously leaving a note for her mother, summarily informing her that one day she would become the world champion of women's surfing. "That was just a bullshit line I fed my mom," she recalls. "I didn't even know a world champion existed in the sport. But I wanted to make leaving home sound good – that I was doing it for a good reason. And then there was a small part of me that wanted to be the best." Such confidence and determination was characteristic of the young champ to be, and she spent the next few months working hard at her surfing, paying her way by working in an Italian restaurant near her new home in Huntington Beach, California. Before long, all the hard work began to pay off.

Lisa ripped through a string of contest wins (she won 35 NSSA trophies in an eight-month period). Naturally, she began to attract a fair bit of notice from the surfing media and it wasn't long before she got entry into the US Amateur Surfing Championships in Florida, in which she took first place. The following year she turned pro, finishing 12th in the world rankings and earning herself the title 'Rookie of the Year'. Over the next few years she continued to make a living from the sport, but it wasn't until 1993, when her daughter Erica was born, that Lisa found her true form. Perhaps driven by the responsibilities of motherhood, from this point on she began to win consistently, finally making good on her promise of becoming the women's surfing world champion in 1994. She then went on to win three more titles, making that a string of four consecutive wins; no other surfer had achieved this since the Australian Mark Richards. In 1996, after winning her second title, she appeared on the cover of the April issue of *Surfer* magazine, making her only the second woman ever to get the cover in the magazine's 40-year history. Such credentials made her not only the most successful female surfer ever up to that point, but one of the world's most successful professional surfers full stop.

Inevitably, most of the people Lisa surfed with in her formative years – and all of those she looked up to – were male, something that has had an obvious effect on her surfing. Indeed, it is often stated that Lisa Andersen surfs like a man. At the time – the mid-1980s – when grace rather than power was the main consideration in women's surfing, this was something of an oddity, but such has been the extent of Lisa's influence on her sport that the aggressive, powerful style she pioneered has now become the norm. In an article in *Outside* magazine, Martha Sherrill wrote: "Within the anachronistically macho world of surfing, respect comes when you rip like a man and act like it's no big thing. Two-time world champion Lisa Andersen is the first woman to pull this off, changing the way beach boys look at beach girls and bringing droves of young women to the sport."

Power, balance and grace: the perfect combination.

Actual, surfing style wasn't the only thing that Andersen influenced. Eschewing the traditional bikini in favour of a pair of men's-style baggy surf shorts, she brought a whole new look to women's surfing too. She signed a few sponsorship deals in the late 1980s with companies such as Billabong and Ocean Pacific, but it wasn't until she hooked up with Quiksilver's women's brand Roxy that things began to change. Lisa was instrumental in the company's development of shorter, more feminine-looking board shorts, simultaneously becoming the face of Roxy, defining a whole new style and helping to create what essentially became a fashion craze – although, with characteristic modesty, she plays down the extent of her involvement in this. Nevertheless, her incredible ability and distinctive style both in and out of the water, combined with the fact that she was a single mother, changed the face of the sport and made her a source of inspiration to a new generation of young female surfers.

And what of Lisa Andersen today? After giving birth to her second child, Mason, in 2001, she has settled in Florida. She made a return to the competitive arena for the 2000 season, finishing fourth despite missing the final two events. She also won the Billabong Pro in Anglet, France. The extent of her future involvement in competitive surfing remains uncertain. But whatever she decides to do next, you can be sure that you haven't heard the last of Lisa Andersen.

Profile: Kelly Slater

"Kelly Slater was abducted by aliens at an early age" reads his profile on Quiksilver.com, "and had a device implanted on his brain that makes him the most competitive sumbitch on two feet." Clearly this is hyperbole but as Kelly Slater is so 'out there' in terms of his surfing, life and fame, who knows what to believe? Here, for example is a guy who can say "I was almost in the film *Charlie's Angels*. I was going to be one of the bad guys who gets killed at the beginning. But I decided not to do it." And it doesn't sound wierd. The strangest part in all this is that most people would read that and think "oh yeah I guess that's what it's like being Kelly Slater". More or less, they'd be right. But it hasn't always been so bizarre.

Born in Cocoa Beach, Florida on February 11, 1972, Kelly, along with mum and brother Sean, had a less than idyllic lifestyle. Although the town they lived in was the epitome of settled suburbia, the Slaters were constantly on the bread line. "I came from nothing as far as money is concerned. My family couldn't pay bills." But if the home life wasn't perfect, the waves outside were another matter; Kelly reckoned they were perfect for him." If I had the choice of learning in Florida or Hawaii, I'd choose Florida," he said in a recent interview. And learn he did.

At just eight years old, Kelly won his first big contest. At ten, he won several East Coast titles and at twelve, he took home his first national prize. His teen years were spent surfing. Magazines started to notice his riding style and he was soon tipped for greatness. He and brother Sean even got sponsored in 1985 by Sundek Surf Shorts. In total he won six Eastern Surfing Association and four national titles before he was 15. While he was obviously on the up, at home he was still just a kid. Perhaps a changing

moment came when he turned 18 and won his first major contest, netting him a cool $30,000 in one go. "I was starting my senior year in high school and I didn't have any friends who had anything over a $5-an-hour job," says Slater now. "It was a pretty radical time. Next thing you know I'm carrying three hundred $100 bills. It was all in cash. I had them laid out on the floor."

After graduation, a fierce bidding war erupted between various manufacturers vying to sign Slater to endorse their brands, and Kelly progressed onto the world tour circuit at 20. In his first year, backed by Quiksilver in what is now one of the longest-running surf sponsorships, he became the youngest surfer ever to win the tour, just after his 21st birthday. It was to be the first of six world championship titles, making him the most succesful competitive surfer ever.

What made his wins even more spectacular was the way in which he set about taking them. As well as cleaning up at nearly every contest he entered, Kelly had invented a new way of surfing. His brand of attacking, inventive and mind-bending surfing made most of the other surfers look dated in comparison. During heats he garnered a reputation for holding back until the final few minutes when he would suddenly unleash himself and win by huge margins. Was he surfing against the other surfers or simply toying with them like a cat would an injured mouse?

It was hard to tell. And while it seemed like his competitive surfing was out on a limb, his personal fame was unquestionably unlike that of any surfer before him. Perhaps it was because he is pretty much the most marketable surfer to have ever entered the sea – after all, *People Magazine* voted him as one of the '50 Most Beautiful People' to have lived – or maybe it was because he could carry himself off as an eloquent, reasoned and intelligent man to anyone who met him. Whatever the reason, his fame transcended the sport. In surfing he was not only the best but by far the best known. Outside of surfing he was the probably the only surfer to have ever become a household name. For a time, he almost *was* surfing.

With nothing more to prove he set about trying to beat his own goals. Big wave surfing was the next arena to be conquered. "Big waves aren't what I do all the time," he said, but despite such false modesty he's surfed Mavericks, one of the most hardcore big waves on the planet, and won the prestigious Eddie Aikau Memorial event at Waimea, Oahu, in waves over 30 feet high.

Out of the water he decided to try his hand at acting, landing the role of Jimmy Slade on *Baywatch* – the most popular show on earth at the time. "I appeared on seven shows over 1992 and 1993. I played a surfer. The problem was I was trying to juggle being a professional surfer – and being taken seriously, while being on this kooky show. So it was a real juxtaposition for me. My heart wasn't in it and it didn't feel like me, so I quit." Although his heart may not have been in the acting, it did introduce him to the show's star, Pamela Anderson, with whom he had an on/off relationship in the years that followed.

By the time he was 26, his everyday life having taken on the surreal qualities of a superstar, he decided to quit competitive surfing. "Win or lose, contests can't make or break me" he said. And so he just stopped.

That isn't to say in any way that he stopped surfing. In fact, the truth is that he surfed harder than ever. Of course, the press couldn't get enough of it. Here was the most famous surfer ever, trying to give the Tour a bit of a breather. Instead he went on a different kind of tour – with the band he and two friends formed, named... The Surfers. He says himself, "It was 1998, the most fun year of my life. I semi-retired and I was with Pam. I had the girl and the career and all that stuff."

In a way he could have simply left it there. But there was more to do and he was still

young in athletic terms. Why quit when you're a legend when you can carry on? And so he carried on, dropping back into the ASP Pro Tour every now and again, showing the other surfers he was still boss. Notably, he would turn up to major events like the Pipeline Masters in Hawaii and beat the world champion.

Inevitably, he rejoined the World Cup Tour in 2002 after being given a wildcard by the ASP for his outstanding contribution to the sport. As he said himself, "career-wise, I want to win another world title and wouldn't be doing it if that weren't my objective. But more than that, I want to help improve surfing. Much of my time is spent thinking how I can advance the sport. That's my biggest goal, helping to make positive changes, to raise the level of surfing, and to inspire people to want to beat me."

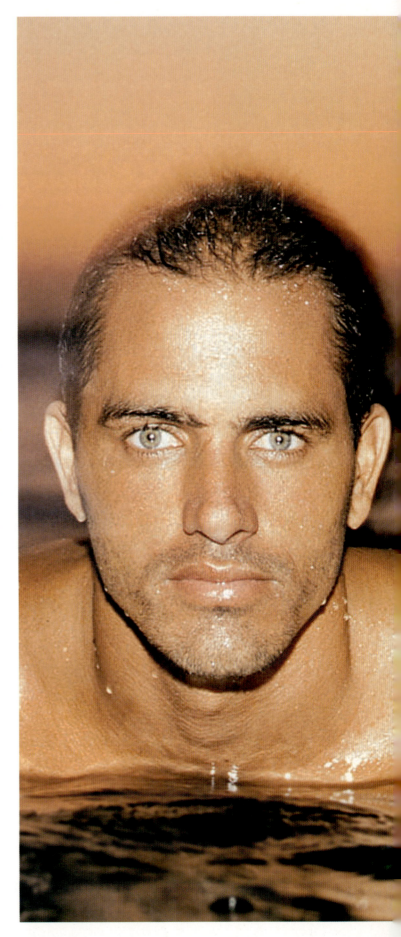

Local brands

Hurley
Established: In 1983, in Costa Mesa by Bob Hurley, making surfboards and partnering up with Billabong Australia.
www.hurley.com

Volcom
Established: In 1991 by Richard Woolcot and Tucker Hall originally as a snowboard brand but have grown into a cross-boardsports conglomerate. Their surf team is one of the best on the planet.
www.volcom.com

O'Neill
Established: In 1952 by Jack O'Neill. After opening his first shop, O'Neill quickly established himself as the leader in making wetsuits for cold-water surfing.
www.oneill.com

Vans
Established: In 1966 with a shoe called the 'Authentic' and yet to be beaten in the skate/snow/surf industry. Have a serious surf team.
www.vans.com

Local shaper

Al Merrick
Established: In 1969, Merrick's company Channel Island Surfboards has been behind most of the great champions in the last three decades. The familiar three-hexagon sticker is often seen on the boards of Kelly Slater, Lisa Andersen and Rob Machado.
Kind of boards he makes: Everything, but known mostly for his cutting-edge thruster three fins.
www.cisurfboards.com

Deep turns & aggressive cutbacks are popular.

AUSTRALIA
& NEW ZEALAND

. AUSTRALIA. 54

By the end of the 19th Century, Australians born and bred on the continent were starting to find their own identity. Unlike their European ancestors (and we're talking here about the modern population of Australia as opposed to the aboriginal population), they had little fear of the sea and were starting to see the Victorian values of modesty, decency and covering up the flesh as fairly redundant. After all, they lived in a country where most towns were within walking distance of good beaches and were baked in glorious sunshine for most of the year – and where it was far too hot to wear stuffy suits that were fashionable on a continent with a different climate. Indeed, it's incredible that such hopelessly inappropriate conventions lasted as long as they did. Up until the end of the 19th Century, for example, there was even a hand-me-down rule that forbade bathing in the sea after seven o'clock in the morning. In an act that accidentally set the country on the path of self-rule, Australians sought to break this bastion of Victorian values, throw off their clothes and damn well swim in their own sea.

Although people were breaking the swimming law up and down the coasts, the most open challenge to authority came in 1902 when the proprietor of the *Manly and North Sydney News* – a man named William Henry Gocher – informed his readers that he was going to bathe at noon the following Sunday. This act of defiance was the release many swimmers were waiting for. In November of the following year, the local council repealed the law restricting sea access. From then on, most Australians were free to take to the waves – and they did so in droves.

1970s tube riding at its best.

With quality waves relentlessly hitting the coast from nearly every angle, it didn't take long for people to become acquainted with the sea's pleasures. Alick Wickham, who arrived in Australia from the Solomon Islands some time in the 1890s, showed Aussie swimmers how to front crawl, a style that later became synonymous with the country, and with this powerful swimming style, Australians soon learned how to play in their waves. Even before the laws on swimming were overturned, a Polynesian boy named Tommy Tana showed locals around Sydney how to master the skill of body surfing. It is widely speculated that it was the spread of this sport that prompted Gocher to publicize the ridiculous swimming restrictions. People wanted to go in the water to ride the waves but they were unable to. He needed a cause to champion and this was it.

With so many young and old Australians out enjoying the sea, it clearly wouldn't be long before someone found out about the Polynesian sport of stand-up surfing. Regular sea trading with Hawaii had begun and the sport was making a comeback there, so it was only going to be a matter of time before someone brought a board back and made a fortune. Enter Charles D Paterson of Manly who, in 1909, returned from Hawaii with a huge redwood board. Unfortunately, his attempts to ride the thing proved unsuccessful and it eventually ended up as an ironing board at the family home, but he had started something: a couple of local kids were inspired to make their own boards and give the sport a go themselves. In fact, Alick Wickham had also tried to instigate stand-up surfing by making a board in Australia even before the turn of the century, but like Paterson's attempt it was destined to fail. Evidently – as with the initial unsuccessful attempts to get the sport off the ground in the USA – for surfing to succeed it needed a big name to push it, and a huge publicity stunt to get everybody's attention. Peterson and Wickham could provide the raw materials, but they had neither the skills nor the fame to give the sport a splash of publicity. In 1914, however, a man arrived in Australia who had more than enough credibility and skill to do just that. And he set about doing it in quite some style.

But first, we need to go back a few years. On August 12, 1911, the sporting world reacted with astonishment when Duke Pau Kahanamoku took more than four seconds off the world record for the 100 yard swim. The event, held in Honolulu harbour, had been arranged in order to give Hawaii a chance for its swimmers to apply for the US Olympic team. Unsurprisingly, when that US team left for the Stockholm Olympics in 1912, Duke was on the ship. In Sweden, Duke would be competing against Cecil Healy and William Longworth, two Australian swimmers defending their 1908 Olympic gold medals. After cruising through the qualifiers with the two Aussies, he somehow failed to show up for the 100m freestyle final (he subsequently claimed the 24-hour sunshine made him sleep late for the race). Duke had obviously made an impression on the two Australians, however, as Healy refused to swim and held the race back until Duke showed up, arguing that it wouldn't be a true race if the best swimmer wasn't there. This act of sportsmanship cemented the Australian and Hawaiian friendship. But it didn't stop Duke taking the gold medal.

Frontside air.

An Uluru rock lip feathering over.

Having destroyed Australia's hopes to repeat their 1908 golds, this unknown swimmer from the Pacific islands became a huge global star. When preparing for the next Olympics, Australia's coach Donald McIntyre had the brainwave of inviting Duke to come and train, race, and generally hang out with their prospective team. The reasons for this cunning move were two-fold: as the current world champion, Olympic medallist and world record holder, Duke would certainly push the limits of the Australians. Moreover, Duke had invented his own style of swimming – the modern-day front crawl – and it was said that his scissor kick was in part inspired by Australian swimmers who had visited Hawaii in 1910. McIntyre wanted the Aussies to watch and learn this new stroke, even if their fellow countrymen had had a hand in its invention. Because Duke, Australia and swimming were somehow joined together in the public mind, the idea of having him over was approved at the highest level. It was believed that a visit by this world-famous athlete would generate huge publicity and spur the Aussies into action. They weren't wrong.

Duke arrived on December 14, 1914, and was housed near the beach of Freshwater. His arrival had been preceded by posters showing him riding a surfboard, from a publicity shot taken from an exhibition poster from Hawaii. This picture had the effect of making people as keen to see him surf as they were to watch him swim. So either on or around Christmas Day in 1914, a mere two weeks after Duke had arrived, a surf demonstration was organised at Freshwater. Unaware of the board Paterson had already imported, Duke built his own with the help of a local timber merchant. On December 23, he gave his first demonstration to a packed beach, taking with him a 15-year-old girl named Isabel Letham for a tandem ride. He got more news coverage than the war in Europe.

Hands in the wave style layback.

What was so unique about the subsequent rush of people into the waves was the fact that elsewhere around the world, the sport stayed within a framework of respectability all the way up until the Second World War, when it began to be regarded as part of the counterculture. The difference in Australia's surf history was that even after the war, Aussies still liked to surf and to be members of their local life-saving club; it appears that surfing never stopped being a respectable sport in Australia. Perhaps this is because even during the war people with good life-saving skills were always in very high demand. Because surfers tend to be the most competent of swimmers, and because most Australians live close to the sea, this attitude of being part of a surf or swim club has prevailed throughout the years.

New Zealand

When the Maori reached Aotearoa around 1000 AD, it is almost certain they brought the ancient Polynesian sport of surfing with them. Whether it had developed into the fully-fledged standing-up variety we can only speculate, but we know for certain that it did manage to transform into a very old version of sledge riding, which would indicate that they had learned to ride standing up.

Regardless, with the invasion of the island by European powers from the 1600s onwards, such indigenous pursuits were doomed. By the 1870s Henry Brook Adams, a writer who had spent time with a Maori Chiefess called Arii Taimai lamented the days when "the shore swarmed with thousands of men and women caring for little but amusement, crowds were always in the water, riding the never-ending surf which seems nowhere else so much at home."

As in other Polynesian islands however, the sport was rejuvenated after Duke Kahanamoku, the Olympic gold medal swimmer and father of modern surfing showed the world the benefits of this regal sport. Following on from his visit to Australia, Duke arrived in Wellington on February 24, 1915. As in Australia, he put

Billabong adverts proclaimed 'Only a Surfer Knows the Feeling'.

on swimming exhibitions, and showed astonished crowds his surfboard riding prowess at Lyall Bay and Wellington on the North Island, and New Brighton and Christchurch in the South. From then on, the movement to the beaches was similar in model to that in Australia. Life-saving clubs were set up from 1932 onwards, and the twin attractions of beautiful coastline and great waves had the sporting population heading for the beach in droves.

In the late 1950s, when surfing was on the cusp of a worldwide explosion, Kiwi surfers were already using similar boards to their US, Hawaiian and Australian counterparts. By the early 1960s, practically everyone wanted to surf.

Today, Aotearoa is world renowned for incredible surf, notably Raglan, Shipwrecks and The Bluff beach breaks. The Maori population, proud of their roots and unique among the Polynesian population in having the treaty of Waitangi (which sets out a contractual agreement between the white settlers and the original owners of the land) have taken surfing as one of their main cultural landmarks, and as such, cover the good breaks with a kind of cultural insurance policy. This, combined with the country's famous love of sport, and growing reputation as the world's spiritual home of everything 'extreme', means surfing has a unique, protected and wonderful home in a beautiful corner of the world.

Generating speed is the mark of an expert surfer.

Surf Spot: Narrabeen

It would be hard to choose one wave to hold above all others in Australia. After all, this is a country with approximately 1,600 miles (2,560km) of surfable coastline – half of which is in water warm enough to surf without a wetsuit all year round. Add to that the fact that 75 per cent of Australians live on the coast and you're looking at a veritable surfing nation. In fact, it is estimated that there are 1.2 million surfers in the country. With so many waves, and so many Aussies to ride them, it's not surprising that many centres around the country claim to have the best beaches, the best point breaks and the best reefs. To be honest they're probably all right – after all, how could you compare Noosa Heads, Burleigh, Kirra, Lennox Head, Angourie, Crescent Head, Seal Rocks and Shark Island against each other, never mind other breaks around the world? Put simply, Australia is probably the most naturally blessed surf continent out there.

So when it came to deciding a wave that summed up the Aussie spirit, we chose not to go on wave size, or ferocity, or consistency, but instead tried to find a wave that was obviously world class, but had something extra, some of the 'X' factor, and something that was uniquely Australian. To complement the Aussie psyche it would have to be fun, serious, loveable but ultimately a bit rogue-ish. It would clearly need to be a place that loves to party too. The choices quickly whittled down to one: Narrabeen, northernmost of Sydney's Northern Beaches, New South Wales.

Narrabeen is an area rather than just simply a one-surf break. In fact, it features many waves of varying degrees of difficulty, levels of danger and amount of localism. It is a peninsula comprising a three-mile stretch of sand, with Collaroy Beach to the south and the rocky Long Reef to the north. In between sit numerous beach breaks all under the Narrabeen umbrella.

The peninsula juts out into the Pacific Ocean, mopping up most eastbound swells that roll in from South Pacific storms. Famously, when these swells hit from an east/northeast swell, they jack up creating some serious barrels that can peel for up to about 900ft (300m). The breaks of North Narrabeen, Little Avalon, Dee Why Point, Little Narrabeen, Long Reef, Gardens and Mona Vale make up the peninsula's best surf spots. Although each has its own characteristics, generally speaking the area creates a sand-bottomed wave, the swells, tides and changing seasons can shift the sand structure and align the wave in different ways. Unlike a point or reef break, which generally breaks in a uniform and predictable way, this shifting sand can make for some unpredictable close-out sets, as well as some epic barrelling lefts. You never know what you're going to get. Locals like to see a south swell hit, which forms a handy rip that pulls surfers out to a line-up like a conveyer belt, called The Alley.

Surf Spot: Raglan

New Zealand has a climate and coastline not dissimilar to Europe. But while the cliffs and beaches may look familiar, the swells that pump in from the storm-ravaged 'Roaring Forties' in the Southern Ocean give it a surfing edge that Europe can only dream about. As trains of swell from this region hit the two main islands, they tend to wrap around points or headlands to create huge curving point breaks, the most famous of which are undoubtedly to be found on the west coast of the North Island.

Head around 50 km west of the town of Hamilton and you'll come across the commune of Raglan, a quiet, unassuming town with an arty, hippy vibe. For surfers however, it is world famous for its incredible surf territory. Head west from the town to find Wainui Beach, a lovely horse-shoe bay beach break that can hold great waves. A few kilometres further and you'll find Manu Bay — often called 'The Point' — said to be the longest and most consistent left hand point-break in the world. Certainly it is a hollow, tubing wave that can mesmerize world-class surfers. A few minutes West of Manu Bay is another peeling left-hander, this one called Whale Bay. While Manu pits spitting barrels, Whale Bay holds its face, producing exhilarating rides section after section. Just watch out for the ever-present rock named — as it should be — 'The Rock' just below the surface. As if that wasn't enough, keep on the western trail where Raglan serves up yet another world beating left-hander a few more kilometres on from Whale Bay called Indicators. Like Manu Bay, this is a harsh, steep, barrelling wave that should keep even sponsored surfers on their toes. As long as they're goofy footers of course.

Such waves have forged and created champions. From the offset Narrabeen was the favoured surf spot for many Sydneysiders. When spiralling house prices forced workers farther out of the city, Narrabeen's population soared. This Aussie working-class undercurrent has prevailed, meaning Narrabeen has a harder edge to it than the more touristy beaches of Bondi and Manly and as such has cultivated a grittier breed of surfer. Perhaps this is the attraction for the younger, keener surfers, but whatever the reason, there's no mistaking the fact that the tubes in this area have spat out some incredible surfers, ably equipped to take on the World Championships with ease. Occy, Tom Carrol, Damien Hardman, and Pam Burridge have all gone more or less from Narrabeen's beaches to tour the globe and take world titles, while recent rippers Joel Fitzgerald, Nathan Webster, Nathan Hedge and Mark Bannister have flown the Narrabeen nest and are aiming for similar glory.

Like it or not, this wave is going to tube.

A tucked in barrel — the perfect water shot.

Profile: Mark 'Occy' Occhilupo

It's June 16, 2004, and Mark Occhilupo is celebrating his 38th birthday with his wife Mae and son Jay on Australia's Gold Coast. Life's pretty good for Mark – he'd spent the morning and early arvo trying to get barrelled at his nearby break of Snapper Rocks, eventually getting tubed in the afternoon session. Now he's had a couple of beers and is looking forward to spending the afternoon in the casino throwing a few chips on the roulette wheel. Whether he wins or not isn't of any major consequence: he's a wealthy surf star, still capable of winning events and giving the World Championship title a serious run for its money. He's also recently re-signed to his long-term sponsor Billabong with a healthy ten-year contract in the bag. It makes him the surfing world's longest running sponsored rider (he's been with them since 1983). On top of the security this contract gives him, in his home country he's been virtually deified, known to surfers, football fans, rugby lovers and anyone with a TV. He's also generally considered to be one of the nicest, most down-to-earth blokes you could ever have the fortune to meet. Life, it would seem, really couldn't get much better.

How that happened, of course, is an absolute mystery. If he'd followed the path that most people thought he'd take, Mark Occhilupo would probably be a washed-up old sports star who took the wrong forks in the road and blamed everyone else for his mistakes. After all, in an earlier incarnation he was a man on a path to self-destruction. A man whose surfing style – full of twisting, unpredictable energy – was nothing compared to the way he lived his private life. Rarely – in or out of the ocean – was Mark Occhilupo ever described as calm or peaceful. His nicknames of 'Raging Bull', 'The Animal' and 'Beast' were as much to do with his lifestyle as they were with his surf style. When 1988 came around, and Mark was generally considered to have finally burned out in a veritable blaze of glory, you wouldn't have found a surfer in the world who would have believed he'd be able to make a comeback. Clearly, when this man went down, people expected him to stay down. The odds of him winning again were unfathomable.

Occy at Sunset Beach in Hawaii. A strong combination.

Born in 1966 in the Sydney district of Kernell as the youngest child to an Italian father and Kiwi mother, Marco Luciano J Occhilupo had what could be described as an idyllic childhood. He grew up with three older sisters in a loving family, ate healthy home-cooked food and crucially, at least for our story, had almost unlimited access to the breaks around the Cronulla peninsula just on the south side of Botany Bay. It was the perfect place for a burgeoning surfer grom. "I'm baffled by the benefits that have been given to me for surfing," he admitted in an interview a few years later. A seemingly insatiable appetite for surfing led him to develop a unique style – one part pure energy, one part speed and several parts style. But if his surfing was untouchable, one thing had to change – clearly, his name was too much of a mouthful for the Aussie palate, and was shortened to 'Occy' early on in his life. It hasn't changed since.

At 13 he won his first amateur comp, quickly following it up with two state titles. At 16 he left school, joined the World Cup tour and earned mythical levels of kudos from everyone who saw him surf. "He was the most exciting unknown surfer I'd ever seen," said Hawaiian surf photographer Aaron Chang when he visited Cronulla in 1983. "I took some photos back to *Surfing* [Magazine] and told them this was the next superstar."

Once on the tour, his explosive surfing made all the introductions the other surfers needed. After making it to 16th place in '83 he shot to 3rd in '84, 4th in '85, and 3rd in '86. Clearly he was in line for the World Championship title. Only one problem stood in his way – US surfer Tom Curren.

The approach and style of the two surfers couldn't have been more different. At the tender age of 16, Occy had made a huge entrance at Pipeline in Hawaii by taking on one of the biggest waves of the winter on his first session at the famed and dangerous wave. Whereas Curren was calculated, powerful and lithe, Occy was fearless, brutish and dynamic; the bull versus the tiger. This made for some incredible contest moments throughout the 1980s, during which Occy's personality, guts and style enamoured him to audiences worldwide – it was said that he had as many fans in Hawaii and the USA as he did back home – a feat rarely, if ever, matched by other surfers. Unfortunately, throughout his bouts with Curren, he'd never won the world title.

By 1988, however, it all appeared to be over. His star had shone so brightly so quickly, but it now already appeared to be on the wane. He ended the tour in that year in 45th place. By '91 he'd slipped to 183rd. Although he was called upon to appear in Jack McCoy's seminal films of the era – notably 1992's *Green Iguana*, which left viewers with no doubts as to his natural talent – everyone thought his contest days were over.

It was said that Occy spent a year on the sofa 'contemplating', eating, drinking and generally letting himself go. Whatever demons were eating him inside, he was trying to placate them with trips to the fridge. Inevitably, he got pretty big.

McCoy came to his rescue. What words of encouragement were said can only be guessed at, but over the following few months, Jack and Occy jumped ship to Western Australia where, under a strict regime, Occy lost 75lb (33.75kg) – almost five and a half stones. He was surfing with his old style, poise and energy, but, incredibly, was now said to have found he had more speed than he'd previously thought. McCoy – filming the story for what would eventually become a video release titled, not surprisingly *Occy: The Occumentary* – had cranked this once-powerful engine back into life. And when it started firing again, there was even more torque than before. All the film needed was a happy ending, and for this to happen there could only be one possible scenario – Occy would have to go back on the world tour. It was 1995 and Mark Occhilupo was ready to give it a fair go.

That year saw him back on electrifying form, finishing a respectable 20th on the tour but more memorably making the Pipeline Masters final, which with Kelly Slater and Rob Machado battling it out is now widely regarded as the best surf final ever. In 1997 he improved yet again, finishing 2nd on the tour behind a seemingly unbeatable Slater. The year 1998 cruised by, with Occy defying athletic principles by staying at the leader board at an age when by rights he should have been thinking of retiring. If '98 was good, then unbelievably in 1999, after a full 16 years on and off the tour, he finally took the title that had been so elusive throughout his career, becoming world champion with one event to spare, at the age of 33.

You would have expected Occy to have quit there and then. And yet he carried on. It hasn't been in vain, either – in the following five years he has continued to win events, dominate heats and worry the championship title race. He's also making inroads into the future of the sport. Billabong, keen to explore new avenues and nurture their very own living legend, have set up the Occy Grom Comp, a four-day exposition of Australia's future surfers overseen by the man himself. Clearly they're thinking of what he can do when he eventually retires from the tour itself. But with results still on the up and with Occy himself saying, "I'm feeling good! I'm not making any calls – but definitely feeling good," it would be crazy to take him off a winning streak. Considering his track record of rewriting the books in terms of what is achievable for older surfers, we can't imagine it's something that's ever occurred to him or his sponsors.

Occy showing a grace under pressure by stalling inside a massive tube.

On top and in control of the waves at Maui, Hawaii.

Profile: Layne Beachley

It's 2003 and Australia's Layne Beachley is sitting on the beach on the Hawaiian island of Maui, thinking about what to do. Losses in the previous two competitions on the women's world surfing tour have meant the five-time world champion is now staring down the barrel of defeat in this last date on the tour. The results would have a profound effect on Beachley's championship campaign. If she were to lose here, she would almost certainly be forced to hand over her crown to Hawaii's own Keala Kennelly. For such a determined and proud competitor, it isn't a good moment for Layne. Previously in the year she'd been troubled with thoughts that after more than a decade on the tour she might have finally burnt out, having neither the will nor the killer instinct to carry on. She'd tried everything, including therapy, to get that stoke on competitive surfing back. What the heats' results proved more than anything was that none of it was working.

"I was sitting there thinking, Oh maybe I need a break and maybe I'll just take the next year off or something," said Layne in an interview after the competition. "I was going through this whole process in my head."

'Burning Out' is a condition well documented within the annals of sport. Take any good athlete and send them on any of the World Cup circuits in virtually any sport and they'll eventually lose the hunger to win. Constant travel, loss of drive and complacency mean that the older stars can sometimes be comprehensively defeated by hungry, eager newcomers. It is the cycle of sporting heroes. On that beach in Maui, Beachley, an intelligent and thoughtful character, cannot have helped but notice that this cycle was closing in on her professional career. But for Beachley, giving up wasn't an option.

Such determination has been a characteristic of this blonde Aussie since her first surfing competition at the age of 15 at her home beach of Manly, near Sydney. State championships followed, then a couple of national competitions and then it was straight into the heady World Cup tour, where fellow Aussie Pauline Menzer took the limelight off Beachley's first win – the prestigious Diet Coke Surf Classic at Narrabeen, Australia – by winning the 1993 World Championships in the same year. While Layne took the whole thing on the chin – she said at the time that it was "more relief than anything, to have finally won an event" – the die was cast: Beachley could and would win events, but there would always be someone else there to slightly overshadow her glories.

Pauline's victory was nothing compared to the following five years' championship campaign, which saw Layne constantly beaten by Florida's Lisa Anderson. The surf press painted Layne as bridesmaid to Lisa's bride, claiming she didn't have the finesse or style to beat the Floridian, and couldn't compete against her savvy comp ways. In this they were probably correct – competition surfing requires not just good surfing but calculated moves designed to give the judges what they're looking for. Layne's speciality wasn't to clock up points; she was more concerned with charging out in the big waves where the freeriders roamed. In this respect, she was in a class of her own.

Thus, in the serious and heavy waves of Hawaii's North Shore, Layne Beachley garnered a reputation for taking on huge waves and surfing them well. "I used to love surfing Waimea," she said in a recent interview, "and going body surfing at Sunset Beach when it's huge and onshore. Just for a laugh."

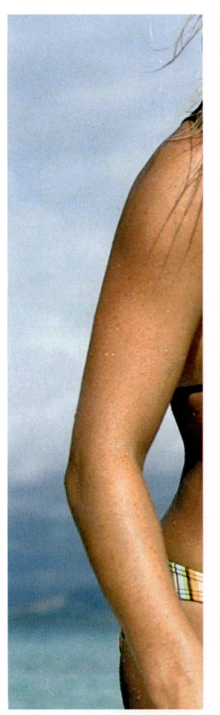

Layne choosing a board on the Indonesian boat trip.

While this would have been enough recognition for most girl surfers, Layne couldn't shake the feeling that she deserved to be a world champion too. Unfortunately, the overall title still eluded her. In 1998 however, Anderson quit the tour for family reasons, which gave Beachley a free road to take her first championship title. She took the win in some style in France the same year. "My shoulders sank to about my knees after winning in Hossegor and then sealing it in Lacanau," says Layne. "It was like, thank God it's over, because now I can claim myself as being a world champion rather than just talking about wanting to be."

Commentators put part of her success down to the fact that Anderson's retirement had conveniently taken Layne's most serious rival out of the equation. But this attitude started to change after she then took the next four titles in a row, equalling Anderson's run of winning five championship campaigns in sequence. By now, Layne had obviously sussed the complicated game of cat and mouse with the judges and the other competitors. So when 2002 rolled around, with Lisa Anderson deciding to rejoin the tour, a 'Rocky'-style re-match of the two champions was on the cards, promising the most interesting tour for women's surfing in years. With deft surfing and calculated style, Beachley not only showed Anderson how much she'd learned, but walked away with the title too. With five consecutive world championships to her name, there was no way anyone could claim Beachley hadn't proved her worth for good.

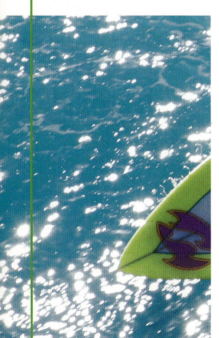

"I went for five from the moment I'd won one," said an ecstatic Layne after the win. "Equalling Lisa's record was a dream come true, but now bettering it is just beyond belief. I don't know what I'm in for now."

And this is where we rejoin her – back in Honolua Bay, Maui, having realized that what she was 'in for' was the toughest test of her career yet. Aching for her title, the other girls are pushing harder than ever and Layne is having an internal struggle with her own demons. "I can just get through this heat," thought Beachley to herself, "just be really fatigued for 20 minutes and give it everything I've got, I can do it right here."

In the end, Layne's surfing wasn't enough to pull her through, meaning it would be down to how the others did to decide the eventual winner. If Keala Kennelly won the comp, Layne would have to let go of the title. It was looking likely that this was the way the cookie was about to crumble.

Feeling the g-force after a strong bottom turn and a fast lip manoeuvre.

But incredibly, the luck that had seemingly always evaded Layne throughout her career now showed up. Keala lost her heat, giving Layne the championship by default. When the points tally confirmed this, Layne realized she'd won her sixth consecutive title, meaning she wasn't just the best ever female surfer, but the most 'winningest' consecutive surfer ever — male or female.

"I couldn't believe it," she said afterward. "I cried. It was just unbelievable. It was just such an emotional victory for me because of how I was feeling this season."

In typical style, it's still not enough. Since her record win, Layne has continued to push the envelope, going out to surf Australia's Phantom Reef with boyfriend and legendary big-wave surfer Ken Bradshaw. "She was interested in tow-in surfing and she adopted it so rapidly," says Ken. "She's such a confident person that she adapted to it quickly."

Layne plays down the role as tow-in pioneer for the girls. "It scared the daylights out of me at first," she says in her Aussie twang. But if it was fear that stopped her, it was her competitive nature that also made her go out for the first time: "It's the fear factor. That's what draws you to it but also what makes you respect it."

Now in her early thirties, and with six world titles under her belt, Layne could afford to be complacent about her future. As you would expect, though, she's not happy to leave things that way. "Personally I still feel like I haven't peaked in my surfing ability. I still feel like I have several years left in me. I want to do it forever."

Local brands

West
Established: 1982 by Patrick Leahy and Roger Liley. One of the most hardcore Aussie surf brands out there.
www.west82.com

Quiksilver
Established: 1970 by Alan Green and John Law, with surf shorts as their first product.
www.quiksilver.com

Billabong
Established: 'Billabong since 1973', as it says on nearly every logo they have. A solid Aussie company with a fantastic surf team including Andy Irons.
www.billabong.com

Rip Curl
Established: In 1967 by Doug 'Claw' Warbrick and Brian 'Sing Ding' Singer in Queensland. Originally made surfboards but moved on to wetsuits and then clothes.
www.ripcurl.com

Coastlines NZ
www.coastlines.co.nz

Local shaper

Matt Manners, Jeff McCoy, Luke Egan, Al Bryne
Established: A long time ago
Kind of boards they make: cool ones with round ends

New Wave (Ralph Blake, Steve Johnson, Andy Kinsella)
Established: 1980
Kind of boards they make: state-of-the-art with the most advanced shaping equipment in New Zealand.

Backside surfing at its best.

EUROPE

About to feel weightless after taking on the lip of the wave.

History

By rights, surfing in Europe should have developed along similar lines to the way it grew in America. After all, Jack London's seminal article 'Riding the South Seas Surf' was written with two publications in mind: one was the USA's *A Woman's Home Companion*; the other was the British magazine *Pall Mall*, which published the piece in 1908. However, unlike the USA, Europe didn't have a coastal climate and beach culture as adaptable and ready to accept the sport as places such as California and Florida, which meant surfing on mainland Europe didn't flourish in quite the same way.

To give Europe its due, sliding along for fun was definitely making a name for itself, but rather than choosing wave power, Europe was seemingly more interested in doing so via another radical new sport – skiing. Perhaps the piste pastime was more readily accepted because the continent had mountains and because warm clothes were easier to develop than the kind of wetsuit that could keep a surfer warm in relatively cold seas. Or perhaps it was because Hawaiian antics simply seemed like a world away. Whatever the reason, while the USA and Australia embraced surfing, Europe was more hesitant.

But it is important to note that an interest in surfing was definitely spreading through Europe early on in the 20th Century, as it did on other continents. In 1932, an edition of one British magazine for boys ran a front cover of some surfers with the tag line 'Surf Riding is Fine Fun'; around the same time, London built the world's first wave pool, and magazines and newspapers ran article after article on the sport, in part because of the fantastic imagery that went with it, and helped in no small way by royal visits to the Hawaiian islands by Edward Albert Windsor, the Prince of Wales, in 1920. During his stay, the prince learned to surf from the original beach boy, Duke Kahanamoku.

While Europe's links to surfing were undoubtedly strong, the actual amount of surfing that went on throughout the earlier part of the century was laughably small. Knowledge of the early days of European surfing is so shady that we don't even have a definite fix on who was the first person to ride any of Europe's waves. Because of Hawaiian and British links (Hawaii was originally a British colony) it is very likely that the first surfer was from the UK, and we know for certain that the first surf club was the Island Surf Club of Jersey, which started in 1923.

Maybe another reason for the slow take-up of the sport was the lack of boards or board-building knowledge. Often, European surfers had to design and build their equipment without any accurate references, although sometimes they were helped by chance visits from Australian, American and even Hawaiian riders. Rumours abound of people making their own boards from sketchy photographs in encyclopedias, going out in thick woollen suits at higher latitudes to learn from scratch or turning up out of the blue with huge boards and giving impromptu demonstrations to awestruck beach-goers. That said, it's hardly surprising that the sport didn't catch on and spur a Californian-style culture. At best, the English coast is habitable without a wetsuit for a few weeks in the summer. And wetsuits weren't commercially available to pre-World War Two surfers.

Of course, World War Two put a stop to most developments in surfing. There are a few reports of surf-related activities popping up across Europe during wartime: a few American GIs arranging for their boards to be shipped over to Cornwall; Australians riding here and there when they had the chance. After all, the sport was gaining momentum in many places around the world, and as more and more people travelled, so the sport was taken with them. Peter Crawford, an English actor living in Hollywood (and who later became part of Frank Sinatra's legendary Rat Pack) learned to surf at Malibu. From 1952 onward he took his board on location wherever he went.

After the war, the twin inventions of fibreglass and neoprene really kicked off the surfing boom in Europe. With the dawn of the 50s, surfboards underwent radical changes – particularly in California and Malibu. Shapes, materials and lengths all changed. With these newer, lighter, more manoeuvrable boards, along with a serious improvement in plane travel affordability, the sport of surfing started to race around the globe. When neoprene entered the equation, vastly improving the possibilities of waterproofing and wetsuits, surfers from established areas such as Australia, Hawaii and of course California realized they could surf in the virtually untouched breaks of Europe.

Harbour walls can produce peeling waves.

Modern surfing arrived in Europe via waves of conquistadors. In France, surfing arrived by accident. As a relatively inexperienced surfer, but someone who was *au fait* with the Malibu scene, film screenwriter Peter Viertel would have been an unlikely enough bearer of the sport to another beach, let alone another continent. In the late 1950s, Viertel arrived in Biarritz, on France's Basque coast, with a Hollywood crew to make the film *The Sun Also Rises*, based on the Ernest Hemingway novel of the same name. Realizing there were good waves in the area, he sent for a surfboard and learned to surf in empty waves along with two locals, George Hennebutte and Phillipe Barland. Along with the Frenchmen and his wife, actress Deborah Kerr, Viertel started The Waikiki, the first French surf club. Since then the area has never looked back, and is now the equivalent of southern California to Europe's huge surf empire.

Similar events conspired to bring surfing to the masses on most other European countries. In England, four Australian lifeguards showed up in 1962 with fibreglass boards, skill and the enthusiasm to take on the waves. The crowds on the beach certainly wanted a piece of it. When The Beach Boys and surfing music invaded Britain two years later, the seas around southern England went from being empty to being jammed with surfers in probably the shortest space of time in the sport's history.

Ireland succumbed in much the same way as England. With an explosion of interest in surf culture, three clubs developed simultaneously in Tramore, Rossnowlagh and the Causeway Coast from 1964 onward. Similarly, Spain took to surfing almost instantly; with Biarritz virtually on the Spanish border, surfing simply moved along the coast westward from the northeast corner. By the early 70s, Spain was a fully fledged surfing nation. Portugal, though slower to react to the surfing craze, followed a similar path. It was been estimated that in 1978 there were as few as 200 surfers in this Iberian surfing paradise; today there are tens of thousands and along with the Basque coast it is one of the Europe's premier surf regions. That Europe dawdled when it came to embracing surfing is perhaps best demonstrated by the fact that Germany didn't get its first surf club until 1991, and without the invention of thicker and more elastic suits, it's doubtful that Norwegians and their Scandinavian cousins would have been able to surf their wonderfully blessed coasts at all. And yet today they take to the world-class waves in 6mm suits, often having only killer whales to share the seas with. It may be a different world to the one that originally spurned the surfing movement, but what northernmost tribes of Europe prove unquestionably is that surfing is in everyone's blood. No matter where our ancestors come from.

Surf Spot: Biarritz

Our choice of Biarritz as Europe's surf spot was a pretty easy one to make. This little jewel of a town on the Atlantic has long been synonymous with surfing in France. Situated on the Côte Basque in the country's far southwest, some 11 miles from the Spanish border, it is blessed with an agreeable climate, beautiful sandy beaches and a unique cultural richness due to its position in the heart of the French Basque country.

Right from the outset Biarritz has been a town whose fortunes are linked inextricably with the sea. It had originally been a whaling village, but by the mid-17th Century it seems that the whales finally began to cotton on to the fact that it wasn't the best place to spend their time, and headed farther out to sea. Life became a bit more arduous for the fishermen who made their living from the whales, but things were soon to change. In the 18th Century, doctors announced that the sea at Biarritz appeared to have therapeutic properties, and once the word got round, patients flocked there in their droves to take advantage of the waters' health-giving properties. Mainstream fame eventually arrived for the town in 1854 when Napoleon III's wife, Empress Eugénie, built a palace on the beach, and from that point on Biarritz never really looked back. It became popular with vacationing royals, and before long its position as one of France's premier seaside resorts became indelibly fixed in the public eye.

Cut to the present day: Biarritz is home to the bulk of the European surf industry and figures highly on any list of 'must visit' spots on the surfer's itinerary. With the pounding that the coastline receives from the Atlantic Ocean and the geographical boon of the 'Fosse de Capbreton', it's not hard to see why. A channel of deep water pointing directly at Hossegor (roughly ten miles north of Biarritz), the Fosse is the oft-cited reason that the area enjoys the quality of waves that it does. It pointed at nearby Capbreton until the 18th Century, when Napoleon Bonaparte famously redirected it in an heroic attempt to provide a safer harbour. This worked, though it's unlikely that he knew the effect it would have on the area's waves. Today, Biarritz and its surrounding area is home to some of the best waves in Europe and a thriving surf scene.

A couple of black clouds cast a little shade on the image of Biarritz as a European surfing paradise. Such is its popularity as a summer destination that the crowds can get pretty horrendous, particularly in the town itself. And although once renowned for their beneficial qualities, the days when the waters of the Côte Basque were championed for their cleanliness are sadly gone. Pollution can get pretty bad, and a couple of years ago the beaches were shut due to the large amounts of crude oil washing up there from the sinking of the oil tanker *Erika* in the Atlantic.

The classic Hossegor line up.

European scenery and peeling right-handers: beautiful combination.

But what about the surf itself? There are so many good spots scattered over the vast stretch of beaches that the only real problem for surfers is choosing which ones to visit. Being directly in front of the town, Biarritz's Grand Plage is probably the one you'll stumble across first. Moving a couple of kilometres north to Anglet, there are a selection of tasty beach breaks, a few of them less crowded due to the long walks from the car park. But perhaps the most famous spot is La Graviere, just north of Hossegor. Like many of the local spots it doesn't always work, but when it's on it knocks out some hefty barrels and is always pretty busy as a result. This is presumably why it is chosen as the site for the annual Quiksilver Pro comp. Move a few hundred metres back south and you'll encounter l'Epi Nord – this provides entertainment for holidaymakers on the adjacent Hossegor front, both for the sizeable rights that break in the outside and the punishing shore break you'd do well to avoid. There are so many other spots in the area that we simply haven't space to mention them here, but rest assured you'll have fun discovering them for yourself.

Profile: Gabriel Davies

In many ways Gabriel Davies is the epitome of a European surfer: someone at home in water of any temperature, a rider who's happy with beach, point and reef breaks, an easy-going guy willing to talk to people of any culture, and of course, someone who loves to travel. This adaptability may have been developed by the fact that to surf in Europe is to experience some of the largest temperature ranges and swell sizes of any continent. Put simply, although there are areas of great surf, on the whole it's not easy to be a surfer if you live in Europe.

In this respect Gabe, as most people call him, is even more hardcore than most. Born in Tynemouth in the northeast of England in 1975, it hardly appeared as though fate had a career in surfing mapped out for him. That changed when Gabe was 11 – a chance visit by a family friend who surfed resulted in Gabe and his brother Jesse being taken out into the waves for the first time. The boys were hooked almost instantly, and from then on spent their summers making local trips to surf the underrated northeast coast as well as venturing farther afield to the cleaner waves of Cornwall. In point of fact, the local water quality was far from ideal: "Pollution is really bad in Newcastle," Gabe commented in a recent interview. "There is a lot of nuclear shit around and it makes it dangerous to paddle out."

But the lure of the waves held, and Gabe started to get good – good enough, in fact, to start competing, do well in some competitions and pick up some sponsorship. By the time of his graduation, at the age of 18, he had signed with Quiksilver and was the subject of a BBC video diary, *Wet Dreams*, which was watched by an estimated two million people. When the time came to go to university, Gabe deferred for a year and opted instead to go travelling and see what the world of professional surfing had to offer. As he himself admits, "I'm not sure if I'll ever end up going now."

In the ten years or so since, Gabe has travelled the world to an extent that defies belief. Along the way he has pushed his own surfing through the roof, eschewed the competition scene and ended up becoming a veritable journeyman, sending regular reports back to European magazines to go alongside the fantastic images of far-flung waves. Whether it's covering arctic storms or being there for a tropical monsoon swell, a typical trip will see him gone for a couple of weeks; a few months later and there are pictures of Gabe smiling out of the pages of the surf mags. Because he can also write well about the places he visits, he is perhaps the ultimate surfing photo journalist.

Gabe now spends his time divided between coasts and continents along with his wife Lauren, a respected author. 'Home' now means summers in France and winters in Hawaii, while in between they could be literally anywhere from Spain to the UK, Indonesia or South America.

Gabe Davies, a long way from home but safely in his element.

Clearly, taking his own surfing to new heights has been Gabe's goal from a young age, and although globetrotting is still a part of his life, it's his exploits closer to home that have been getting the column inches more recently. Of late, Gabe has been getting to grips with a secret big-wave venue named G-Spot, somewhere off the Irish coast. Along with long-time friend Richard Fitzgerald, Gabe has been learning to tow in to the wave with the aid of a 1200cc jet ski and a waterski-style rope. This offshoot of surfing is gaining momentum in Hawaii and the Pacific islands, but is relatively new in Europe.

"We're the first to do this in Ireland," Richard recently told the *Irish Independent*, "but that's only because nobody else is mad enough."

Gabe is clearly enthusiastic about the possibilities it's opened up. "With the help of a jet ski we can now get to places that we could never previously be able to reach because they are too far from the coast to paddle out to."

Once there he adds, he can "catch waves that you could never normally catch by using just your arms' paddling power."

After only a few months of exploration, they came back with incredible news of a new, huge wave somewhere off the Irish coast. The spot they've found is geographically under wraps for the time being, but those who've been there are quick to point out its attraction. *Surf Europe* has dubbed it Europe's heaviest wave, and Gabe himself is quick to call on his experience in classically hailed big waves such as Waimea Bay to judge it. "As a professional surfer I've surfed all over the world, but the best wave right now is G-Spot: it's so hollow, so fast and so heavy, right up there as our version of Pipeline, and for me it beats everything else."

Having found a world-class wave in his first year of tow-in surfing, and with Gabe only beginning to enter his prime as a surfer, it looks like the future of surfing in Europe is in safe hands.

Frontside slash action.

Local brands

Revolver
Established: In 2000, Newquay, Cornwall. Stockists of retro, soul and modern surf products as well as being fonts of knowledge.
info@revolversurf.com

Gul Wetsuits
Established: In 1962 by Dennis Cross in Bodmin, Cornwall.
www.gul.com

Animal
Established: In 1987, originally as a watch company for surfers but now a major brand in Europe with clothes, surfboards and accessories.
www.animal.co.uk

Local shaper

Chris Jones
Established: In the early 1960s, after Jones was taught by Billbo founder Bill Bailey. Jones now has over ten thousand boards under his belt.
Kind of boards he makes: From longboards to retro and back. Now runs The Newquay Surfboard Company.
www.surfsup.co.uk

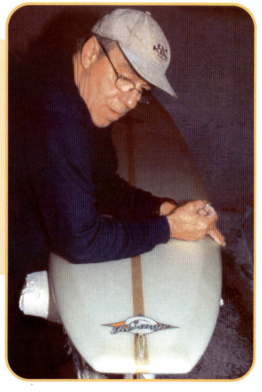

Chris Jones, checking the lines.

Complete control in an ever changing environment.

SOUTH AMERICA

. SOUTH AMERICA. 84

History

By the nature of its geographical and economic position within the world, surfing in South America should have arrived fairly late into the 20th Century on the backs of travelling surfers from more opulent countries. In fact, the continent, and in particular the area of what is modern-day Peru, could have nurtured one of the oldest surf cultures known to man, possibly even older than the established Polynesian origins to which most modern historians trace surfing's roots.

The reason for this is because recent research by The Surfrider Foundation has unearthed remarkable evidence that the fishermen around Huanchaco in Northern Peru surfed their reed canoes, called Caballitos, several thousand years ago, almost certainly pre-dating surfing in the Hawaiian island chain. The evidence is based on local ceramic art decorated by surf-like scenes, murals of point-breaks wrapping around what looks like a surfer and the fact that many of the religious buildings were built either on or very near important surfing beaches.

It isn't the first time surfing roots and ancient Peru's past have criss-crossed. Respected anthropologist Thor Heyerdahl spent the lion's share of his career trying to convince the world that Polynesia had originally been peopled by travellers from South America, citing plants, pottery, art and his own adventurous voyage on a balsa wood raft as evidence to prove the point. His argument is compelling and certainly the modern potato plant made its way from South America to Polynesia a long time before western explorers could have transported it, proving that the two ancient cultures met somewhere. Did they trade surfing secrets? Which one influenced the other? Who surfed first? Most of the evidence still points towards Hawaii as being the root of modern surfing, but if further revelations are forthcoming we may have to revise our surf history in the future.

In the meantime we can trace South America's modern surfing culture back to a specific point in time – and once again, it is Peru that features as the catalyst country. In 1939 a rich sugar magnate's son called Carlos Dogny learned to surf in Waikiki, on the Hawaiian island of Oahu. As luck would have it, the person who turned him on to the sport was none other than the father of modern surfing, Duke Kahanamoku. Like many surfers, Dogny was hooked for life and returned to his native Peru with a board in order to carry on surfing around his home city of Lima.

With time on his hands, and having found the break of Miraflores only 15 minutes from Lima, Dogny and three other Peruvians founded the extravagant Club Waikiki, based around grand traditions in a similar vein, such as yacht clubs or imperial tea rooms. No expense was spared. In 1955 they even invited Hawaiian surfers over for a friendly competition, throwing what is considered to be one of the very first full international meets and quite possibly the genesis for a full world tour. Certainly it opened up interesting cross-cultural ideas for the Peruvians and Hawaiians and an unlikely channel was opened that saw Peruvians and Hawaiians busily swapping shores as the seasons changed. Visiting surfers to Club Waikiki were astounded by the incredible opulence of the place: there were kids to carry your boards, fish ponds, gardens, tennis and squash courts, bars, changing rooms and even hot showers. It was a veritable surf paradise.

By 1965, the surfing contests had finally joined up to make a world championship viable. The very first surfing world champion was Peruvian Filipe Pomar – himself a Club Waikiki member. His win, combined with Club Waikiki's regular invitations to legendary surfers to come and perform, put Peru firmly on the map. When those surfers visited, the parties were legendary, even when the waves weren't pumping. In 1969 Jeff Hakman, fresh from a win at the most prestigious event in the world – the Duke Kahanamoku Invitation at Sunset Beach in Hawaii – went to Lima as part of the prize. When he arrived, the club announced his 'winning duties', which included entering the ring at a genuine bullfight. "I was terrified," said Jeff, in his autobiography, on his encounter with the huge, angry animal. "Then I dropped the cape and ran."

. SOUTH AMERICA. **86**

Clear, clean water. A godsend for any surfer.

Surf Spot: Chicama, Peru

Ask most knowledgeable surfers where the longest wave in the world is and they'll probably all reply, "Chicama". But does anyone know where this mystery nirvana is? And how do mere mortal surfers get to ride it? The rumours say that it's always pumping and always has offshore winds – and every time the tale is told, the wave seems to get emptier and emptier. Could it be true?

Actually, the question that really needs to be asked is: "Why not go and see for yourself?" Because Chicama is pretty easy to locate – it's around nine hours by land north from Peru's capital city of Lima. Buses are frequent and generally speaking the infrastructure in getting around the place is very well organized. There are flights to the nearby town of Trujillo, there are cheap and cheerful surf houses nearby and some spectacular hiking a few hours away. Bizarrely, the rumours that there is hardly anyone around to surf it are in some ways true. In all probability the wave is peeling left in the same perfect way it's done for thousands of years, and at this very moment there'll probably be no one riding it.

Why this should be is a matter of debate among surfers everywhere. Certainly it is not because of the break's infrequency, as this coast is one of the most consistent surf spots in the world, with the almost constant 'roaring forties' storms to the south regularly pushing waves up to the Peruvian coast at a height of around 3–5ft (1–1.5m). Neither is it because the wind is unfavourable – offshore winds dominate the point. And when you consider the fact that this wave can peel for up to 2.5 miles (4km), giving a rider a solid five-minute ride with tube sections and consistent walls, it seems like it should be the most crowded wave in the world. But it isn't.

Most people put its unpopularity down to the fact that the wind, the sea temperatures and the mist that almost permanently blankets the region – along with the dark, bleak sand and landscape – conspire to make the place look uninspiring and uninviting for travelling surfers. It simply looks drab in photos. But can that really be all that puts people off?

What they are missing is spectacular. On good days, most surfers are unlikely to notch up more than a few rides. Due to its length, the wave will take a surfer a long way from his or her starting point. To get back to the take-off point, one faces the choice of either paddling – which would be a huge chore – or to ride the wave all the way to the beach and to walk back along the sand. Not unsurprisingly, everyone takes the beach option, but even then, with a walk of nearly 3 miles (4.8km) for each wave the number of rides a surfer takes is in direct relation to how far he or she can actually walk in a wetsuit.

Another reason that is banded around for Chicama's surprising lack of crowds is the fact that surfers actually get bored of riding for so long. Although this seems incredible, perhaps it does happen. There is also an abundance of equally good and ridiculously long waves in the area – the location and shape of the coast here, which lies a few hundred miles south of Ecuador, creates long, peeling left-hand point breaks. What it lacks is the visible beauty associated with other surf hot-spots and seemingly the only thing one can deduce from the lack of surfers is that as well as good waves, and a comfy place to eat and sleep, surfers also appreciate the surrounding landscape more than has been previously assumed. Or maybe the surfing experience actually relies on a balance between the amount of time spent surfing along the wave and the amount of fun to be had actually dropping in too. Whatever the reason, Chicama should be on every surfer's hit list at least once in their lives.

A classic 'hands behind the back' barrel.

Profile: Flavio Padaratz

Some surfers work their way to greatness; some have greatness thrust upon them thanks to a combination of genes, luck and an unquenchable thirst for surfing and professional achievements that outweighs anything their peers can muster: think Lopez, Curren, Occy and Slater. Others transcend their origins and their personal take on the art of surfing and come to symbolize something else entirely, regardless (although usually because) of their surfing achievements.

Once such surfer is Flavio Padaratz. Take a glance at his results sheet since 1988, when he joined the ASP Tour, and you'll see the proud record (including three Top 10 finishes and two WGS titles) of a modern professional surfer holding his own among some of the more stellar names of the era. But with Flavio, it's all about the context. What these results don't tell is how Flavio was one of the trailblazers for the modern Brazilian professional surf hegemony, opening the doors for the many who have followed in the intervening period. And they don't explain how on earth a kid from a sleepy backwater with no surf culture could initiate such a charge. For that, you have to go back to Flavio's roots.

A big wave, complimented by a big bottom turn.

Although he first came to prominence internationally in 1990, when *Surfer* magazine featured him in their Grom Issue, the Padaratz story began on April 19, 1971, when he was born in Blumenau, a town with no waves and whose website is currently advertising the annual beer festival. It took a decade for surfing to pique the youngster's interest, but once it did his progression was swift. "It was sheer luck," he admitted in a recent interview. He borrowed a board from a kid in his town, took it to Camborlu — an hour from his home — and "right then I got hooked. I realized I could actually ride the thing, and the shit waves at Camborlu were the perfect place for me to learn."

Perhaps it's this legacy of honing his craft on less-than-ideal waves that makes Flavio such a killer in the soup today. Either way, he studied his craft in relative obscurity for a year or so until Brazilian shaper Avelino Bastos offered him a revolutionary deal: he would give him boards, get him into shape and send him to Huntingdon Beach to complete his schooling. In turn, if all went to plan, Flavio would develop into the country's first competing surfer on a world-class level. They were great days for Flavio, and it's a period he now credits with evolving his competitive edge and advancing his surfing. "I became this non-stop surfing machine, which is great because I was surfing good and I earned the respect of all the gringos," he told interviewer Vince Medeiros in 2001.

By 1992, Flavio was in the Top 16 and was notching up some good results; a couple of wins were followed by a run of successful years. But by 1996 things had taken a downward turn. A 46th-place finish suggested something was amiss. Looking back five years later, Flavio put his drop in form down to disillusionment with the punishing travel schedule the pro surfer must follow each year, and the fact that he was no longer having much fun on the tour. For Flavio, enjoyment is a crucial element to his surfing. As he put it a few years later after regaining his place on the ASP: "I'm only up there with the best because I don't surf thinking about the title, about results. I work without expecting to win. If I do win, great but the result is just a consequence of the process." Perhaps it was this fatalistic attitude – a combination of *que sera sera* and a steely surf stoke determination – that enabled Flavio to regain his place once his *annus miserablis* came to an end.

Either way, after a couple of wilderness years on the WQS Tour beset by disastrous arm injuries (courtesy of a drunken fall on a dancefloor and a football mishap), Flavio was back where he belonged on the ASP Tour. It seemed to coincide with a fundamental change of attitude too, with Padaratz swapping his hedonistic habits of yesteryear for a new healthier approach involving yoga, swimming, running and guitar playing. It was an approach that soon paid dividends, and for the next few years one of Brazil's pro surfing pioneers enjoyed results that matched his previous experiences on the tour.

Flavio's pro surfing journey eventually ended in December 2003, at the Xbox Gerry Lopez Pipeline Masters. Losing in his second-round heat against Mick Fanning, the Brazilian took the defeat in his characteristic laissez-faire style, commenting, "Well, I guess that's the end of the 15-year-old round-the-world heat." As *Surfer* commented at the time, it was "the beginning to a new career phase, rather than an end" and today Flavio continues to spearhead the Brazilian scene as a television presenter, co-owner of Tropical Brazil and the licensee of Brazil's WCT event. And, of course, that famous forehand snap is still in evidence.

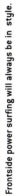
Frontside power surfing will always be in style.

Local Brands

Havaianas
Established: In 1962 as a surf sandal brand.
www.havaianas.com

Reef Brazil
Established: In 1984 by Argentinians Fernando and Santiago Aguerre.
www.reef.com

AFRICA

Cold water, big sharks and huge waves will almost guarantee an empty line up.

A Natal beachbreak rolls on through.

History

Africa's surf origins go back a long way. And as with Peru, there are spots along the continent's west coast that might legitimately challenge Hawaii's claim to be the birthplace of surfing. In the 1830s, a ship's captain wrote an account of some local kids taking to the waves on boards in Senegal, Ivory Coast and Ghana. These reports are almost certainly true, but whether this was a separate development from the surf-riding practised by the Hawaiians at the time is a matter for future historians to work out.

As on every other continent, what we would consider to be modern surfing didn't arrive in Africa until the spread of surf culture in the 20th Century. And even when it did appear, it wasn't taken up by many people on the continent. The fact it hasn't spread all over Africa says much about surfing's status in the grand scheme of things. Africa covers an area of roughly 12 million square miles (31,080,000 sq km) and almost four-fifths of that is surrounded by a coastline blessed with world-class waves. When you add on the fact that it receives swell from the Atlantic and Indian oceans as well the odd storm swell in the Mediterranean and Red seas, Africa becomes possibly the most surfable continent on the planet.

But sadly, its turbulent political climate and lack of central infrastructure has meant that throughout the last century Africa lagged behind the global surf movement in a big way. This is proof positive that surfing can only survive in a climate of social balance and relies on the availability of leisure time that such a climate implies.

More than 100 years after travel reports came back that Africans were into wave riding, Californian film-maker Bruce Brown took two surfers — Mike Hynson and Robert August — on a worldwide surf trip, resulting in the film *The Endless Summer* (1966). The film has now attained seminal status among surfers, not least for its scenes of African villagers following the two surfers to the beach en masse. Everyone in the village wants to try this crazy sport, and local fishermen even take their '3,000 pound' boat on a ride on one wave. Clearly the trio were the first surfers to have reached certain villages by the mid-1960s, but when they reached the southern tip of the continent they encountered an already established surf scene there. How did that happen? Funnily enough, the situation was the same in the north.

If West and East Africa were still remote remote outposts by the 1960s the same can't be said of Morocco, which attracted nomadic surfers eager to branch out from Europe and explore southward. It's easy to see why — with enticing cities such as Marrakesh, the snow-capped Atlas Mountains, endless empty point and beach breaks and a culture so famously open to mind expansion that Jimi Hendrix made a pilgrimage there, it was hard for many surfers to resist.

Although Morocco was certainly a prime surf destination, and indeed part of what most travelling surfers considered the 'European' surf trail, it was to be South Africa that generated its own indigenous surf population. While this was certainly an offshoot from the Australian branch of surfing, it quickly became something quite different from the Aussie surf clubs to the east. For a start, the ugliness of apartheid in South Africa reared its head in the form of segregated beaches. To take just one example, when the Gunston cigarette company invited three surfers over from Hawaii to take part in a series of competitions, two of them — Jeff Hakman and Bill Hamilton — were allowed to surf the white beaches; the third — Eddie Aikau, a pure Polynesian surfer — was turned away from the hotel and the beach he was supposed to compete at because of his darker skin. Clearly, a ridiculous situation.

1970s' kids look on as an early pioneer rides a perfect left hand point break.

The dorsal fin of a great white shark.

If the political problems on the beach were a deterrent for many would-be travelling surfers — and the anti-apartheid movement had always been fairly strong outside South Africa — further causes for concern came from the dangers in the water. South Africa is widely reported to be the Great White Shark capital of the world. That said, some areas might be safer than you actually think. In 1962 Durban started to put up shark nets, and there hasn't been an attack on the netted beaches since. Clearly, there is something to be said for this invention — nearby, the un-netted Amanzimtoti Beach has the worst shark attack record in the world.

These days, with the political situation stabilizing in SA, the country is rightfully emerging as one of the best surf destinations in the world. With nearly 2,000 miles (3,200km) of coastline — including Jeffrey's Bay's famous Boneyards, Supertubes and Tubes, widely regarded as the best right-hander point breaks in the world, and the mellower break of Bruce's Beauties at Cape St Francis (named after Bruce Brown stumbled upon it) — the country has gained a worldwide reputation among surfers.

It looks like the rest of Africa has a long way to go to match South Africa's infrastructure, though. With most of the continent still fairly inhospitable to all but the hardiest travellers, 70 per cent of the population living on under $2 per day and disease a major concern for millions of Africans, luxuries such as surfing look set to remain low down on the list of most people's priorities for some time. If and when the continent emerges from this dark period, Africans can look forward to reaping the rewards of their incredible coastline and travelling surfers will have more or less doubled the amount of waves in the world to choose from.

Surf Spot: Dungeons

With so many famous waves to chose from, our choice for Africa's chief surf spot was always going to be tricky. From Morocco's Castles, South Africa's J-Bay, Namibia's empty Skeleton Coast or Madagascar's unexplored coastline to any one of the breaks on the offshore islands such as Mauritius, Reunion and the Canaries, the scope for wild, varied, incredible waves is seemingly endless.

But if you're looking for just one wave to sum up something unique about surfing in Africa, then the choices quickly whittle down to just one venue: a wave left that breaks on a winter swell underneath a scary-looking mountain called The Sentinel.

The Dungeons line up from Chapman's Point.

South of Cape Town on the peninsula lies the town of Hout Bay. Head out on the M6 and you'll eventually arrive at Chapman's Peak, a look-out stop with unrivalled views across the open bay towards Duiker Island. It was here in 1984 that local surfers Pierre de Villiers and Peter Button sat looking out at an enormous wave breaking in the bay. For the previous year they'd asked other riders in the area if anyone had surfed it, but after exhausting every avenue they came to the conclusion that no one could tell them anything about the place. And yet there it was, this huge wave breaking and peeling with a tantalisingly empty line-up.

There were only two things about it that they could be sure of. Firstly, it was probably two to three times bigger than anything they'd ever surfed. And secondly, because of the massive seal colony on the nearby Duiker Island, there would be Great White Sharks cruising the area. Incredibly, using equipment verging on the laughable, they decided to paddle across the deep-water channel to have a closer look at this seemingly deadly wave.

"There was a powerful stench from the island teeming with seals," said Button in a recent interview. "We paddled around and realized our boards, which were under six feet, were not appropriate. It was all a bit scary that first time."

The idea of paddling a 5′ 6″, twin-finned 80s short-board nearly a mile across the most dangerous water in the world to meet one of the most dangerous waves in the world would be most surfers' idea of pure hell, and yet they went back again and again – sometimes taking other surfers with them, sometimes just going it alone. "We'd park our car there," recalls Pierre. "It was an all-day mission, the climb over the mountain was a good hour and the paddle was a good 20 minutes."

Throughout the 1980s and 1990s, Pierre and Peter – along with Peter's brothers Trevor, Michael and Graham, and local big-wave riders such as Jurgen Rammesmeyer – quietly continued to surf Dungeons alone. Slowly, they got the feel of the place, designing bigger and better equipment, taking on the fierce wave and always being on guard for 'predators'. For some reason, the attraction of the wave was greater to them than the dangers presented by the obvious perils. Tellingly, their youthful exuberance for surfing the wave has now ebbed. With the advent of time, reflection and memories, they realize how much they had actually risked. "I wouldn't do it now," says Pierre. "No way."

By the year 2000, the interest in big-wave riding had progressed enough for the first ever contest to be held on the break, now named Dungeons. Appropriately sponsored by Red Bull, an energy drink and adrenalin substitute, the Big Wave Africa contest gained acceptance when huge-wave experts from around the world gave their stamp of approval to the place. These surfers had ridden the established big-wave venues of Waimea, the North Shore Outer Reefs and California's beast of a wave, Mavericks, and their say-so gave this South African monster genuine credibility. Even though the wave didn't actually peak out at its maximum size, the mountain, the sharks and the sheer heaviness of the place all conspired to make an indelible impression on the competitors.

"Dungeons intimidates me the most out of any wave in the world," said Jamie Sterling, a Hawaiian big-wave charger who was over for the event. "It's a serious wave."

If 2000's event was a fitting entrance into the big-wave arena, it was 2001's Red Bull Big Wave Africa that really put the place on the map. While they were getting to know the peak, several surfers were introduced to one of the wave's real locals when a huge Great White started to harass them.

"It was the biggest thing I've ever seen in the water," said Jason Ribbink, a competitor from Durban, South Africa. "My heart was beating like this," he added, hitting his chest. "It came back four or five times before we could climb into the boat and get out of there. Its dorsal fin was so big it seemed like it was bending from the weight."

Fittingly, with the blessing of the competitors, the decision was made to go ahead with the comp.

"Of course I'll be in there," said Ribbink when asked whether he still intended to compete in the event, adding: "With eight guys in the water you've only got a 12.5 per cent chance that the shark will be interested in you."

Lining up a South African barrel with expert timing.

Have board, will travel.

Profile: Kevin Naughton and Craig Peterson

When Bruce Brown visited Africa he brought back some of the first images of perfect waves, funny locals, strange customs and curious villages. The intrepid spirit of the film captured many hearts in cinemas and living rooms around the world. But Brown's film – an almost comedic snapshot of the continent – was arguably eclipsed by Gregory Schell's *The Far Shore*, an altogether grittier portrait of two travelling surfers who went on to explore vast areas of the continent throughout the 1970s. Their trip was uniquely placed to lift the lid on what the surfing experience in Africa was actually like.

Kevin Naughton and Craig Peterson were two Californian surfers eager to leave the oversaturated waves of their home state to embark on their own journey of discovery. "By the time I became a teenager," says Kevin in the film, "It seemed like it had gotten pretty crowded to me." Craig – a staff photographer for *Surfer* Magazine – approached Kevin on Huntington Beach to ask if he wanted to branch farther out. Little did they know that the trip they were about to embark on would last ten years.

At first they ventured to Central America, where a 16-year-old Craig took pictures of the then 18-year-old Kevin riding some empty points. Throughout their trip they sent rolls of film back to the magazine, with Kevin jotting down notes on their exploits to accompany the text. "For some reason," says Craig, "the combination of photos and words just seemed to work really well." Over the next few years, their stories gained a huge following. Even the editor of the magazine didn't know when or where the next story would come from. But it was eagerly anticipated.

"We had a bit of leverage with *Surfer* Magazine because of the popularity of the articles," says Kevin. "We'd come to them with the idea about going some place. We'd usually get a little bit of front money to actually get us out of the airport. After that we'd send in the photos and the articles and hope there'd be a cheque waiting for us at the next spot. Sometimes there was, sometimes there wasn't."

The realities of this nomadic existence came through the text without actually being spelled out. Here were two guys doing exactly what you could do if you simply walked out of the house and started your own adventure. The fact that they were clearly winging it only made it sound more appealing. Their articles overflowed with enthusiasm for the travelling life. And when they went to Africa in 1974, the primordial beat came right out of the page.

"Beaches," writes Kevin in one piece about West Africa, "are one of the only places that scorpions won't traverse. The air was dry, there was no problem with mosquitoes, so we slept out under the stars. After waking, we showered ourselves on the tail end of a two- to three-metre swell."

While the accounts that made it back were upbeat to reflect the editorial content of the mag, the reality of the situation wasn't as romantic as some of the readers may have supposed. Today, Kevin reflects: "The whole perception of the travel lifestyle we had you know — hanging out on some remote tropical beach under palm trees — just trying to decide when we'd go back out for a surf, maybe after this coconut maybe after the next — that's kind of the image and the way people like to see it but really it can be incredibly difficult for long periods of time."

Surf boards aren't the only method of sea travel.

"Travelling in Africa," Kevin continues, "it's all hard and arduous. It's all that way. Everything you do. Everywhere you go you brace yourself. Every day you're thinking 'Am I going to get sick today? Am I going to eat the wrong thing?'"

Eating things wasn't their only worry. To get to the sea they would sometimes paddle down rivers rather than cut their way through the bush. Often, local villagers would come out and yell "Bill Hazay!" at them. "We thought, Cool there's this guy Bill Hazay who's been here before us with a surfboard. I wonder if we'll get to meet him?" remembers Kevin. What they didn't realize at the time was that Bill Hazay wasn't a person, but a river-based worm called bilharzia that burrows into the skin and kills its victims. "Only much later did we find out it wasn't a he but an it," says Kevin now, laughing.

Inevitably though, Africa did get to them. Kevin got ill, very nearly dying after going down with dysentery in the jungle. "At one point I thought I'd crossed that threshold from knowing that you're seriously ill to wondering if you're even going to survive," he says, shaking his head.

But survive they did, eventually making it through the Sahara Desert, and finding what they had come for. "Suddenly," says Craig, "we came across this trail and there at the end of it was this perfect wave."

Further adventures saw them holed up in a slave fortress, dining on tangerines after stumbling across a fellow surfer in a fully-equipped Land Rover, hitchhiking in the middle of nowhere, stripping naked in the desert and losing themselves deliberately – and, of course, leaping into the sea and riding perfect, empty waves.

"One of the great aspects about travelling is that sense of freedom and free will," says Craig now. "I think that was part of the philosophy that made the trip so much fun."

They left Africa in 1978, having explored for four years across a vast area but truthfully only having scratched the surface of the continent. Their endless cover shots and sensational stories made incredible copy and obviously inspired many of the mag's readers to travel too. Perhaps the most important message they had was that to go travelling wasn't about anything other than the journey itself – certainly no one could accuse them of only doing it for the money. So the question remains: just exactly why did they go to Africa of all places, when there were easier options around the world?

"Well," says Kevin, "I think we picked Africa because more than anywhere else on the planet it was the big unknown and that's what was enticing about it. Plus the idea of finding a good wave off the edge of the Sahara sounded so cool. Just like, 'We gotta do it.'"

Local shaper

Pete Daniels
Spyder Murphy

Pete Daniels checks the finish on another Spyder creation.

ASIA &

INDONESIA

A modern day adventurer on a far-flung voyage.

History

In surfing terms, if Indonesia did not already exist, it would be a fantasy in the minds of surfers everywhere: a surf idyll. 'The world's most perfect waves', 'the world's greatest archipelago' – such descriptions of the conditions in Indo are routine. And yet, the surfing world didn't fully discover the potential of the place until the early 1970s, five hundred years after the earliest recorded description of the fearsome Indonesian line-up. Sure, today the description ("The waves in the ocean were like hills the sound of the breakers thundered as though desirous to completely end the world in the Age of Destruction.") might sound a tad dramatic, but anybody who has been caught inside by a jarring Indo clean-up set might have an idea where Danghyang Nirartha, the priest-poet to whom these words are usually credited, was coming from with his hyperbolic description.

Because Indo is big. We surfers might have caught on late, but once the secret was out the surf industry colonized Indonesia in record time. It happened so quickly that in 1994, 20 odd years after it began, Aussie Jim Banks could reminisce about "a Kuta perfumed with clove cigarettes and chicken sate. It seems that everything we came here for has been replaced by the very things we were trying to escape." The irony – surfers discovering and ultimately ruining a form of Eden – could fill another book. But we do know that the first surfers in Indo were attracted by this idea of paradise. Surf orthodoxy has it that Aussie surfers were the first to make the hop, but the book Surfing Indonesia makes the point that "The original pioneer of surfing in Bali was a colourful expatriate from Los Angeles named Robert Koke." Koke, a Hollywood face and one of those larger-than-life characters that crop up in surf history, had learned to surf in Hawaii. Visiting Bali on holiday, he saw the potential of Kuta and Bali, and built the first surf hotel. He also had the first boards shipped in and, in Christmas 1938, reputedly became the first surfer to paddle out in Indonesia. Like other pioneers, Koke probably had no idea what a Pandora's box he'd opened and the consequences it would have on the paradise he loved. In the late 1960s, Australian surfers began to arrive, bringing modern surfing and its attendant culture to the islands. They felt they'd found surfing's last paradise, when in reality all they had done was hasten its end.

Indonesian surf spots are an explosion of colour and force.

A visit to Indonesia today will set off contradictory feelings in the mind of the thinking surfer. With a staggering 49,600 miles (eighty thousand kilometres) of theoretically surfable coastline (much of it undiscovered), the friendliest people in the world and a local infrastructure that makes surf travelling ridiculously straightforward, Indo is still undeniably paradise for surfers. That said, events in Bali in 2002 and the long-lasting poverty of the people (despite the fact that millions of surf dollars are obviously passing through the country) make it a paradigm for both the best and worst aspects of surf culture. The beach of Kuta that Jim Banks pined for – once a beautiful fishing village, now a thriving surf Shangri-La with a McDonald's on the beach – is only the most notorious example. Time will tell as to how Indonesia will face the future challenges her beauty and uniqueness will attract. Our role as visiting surfers is to put something back into the country that has given us so much.

Surf Spot: Indo Spots

If you begin running the numbers on Indonesia, some surprising statistics come to light. For a start, Indo is the sixth most densely inhabited country on the planet, with a population estimated to be in excess of 200 million. Its indigenous languages run into the many hundreds. The last time anybody bothered to count the total number of islands in the group, they gave up after hitting 13,600. In an archipelago that features so much surfing terrain to get lost in, it's perhaps unsurprising that surfing in Indonesia has evolved its own idiosyncrasies.

Clear water over coral reef can be dangerous.

It's traditional to begin, as the entire scene did, in Bali, which has an embarrassment of breaks to suit all conceivable levels of surfing ability. Purists will sniff, but Kuta has some lively breaks to sample: Kuta Beach, Padma, Blue Ocean, Kuta Reef and – if you fancy getting a good look at the planes landing at Denpasar – Airport Reefs. Further south of Kuta you'll find the strange teardrop-shaped piece of land that hangs from Bali's underside: The Bukit.

The Bukit is usually the surf traveller's first taste of those Indonesian paradise clichés. Beginners and those after a mellow time usually head to Dreamland, a well-named beach settlement, an A-frame with a late, mellow take-off. The good news about The Bukit, though, is that it has a surplus of spots, meaning that Dreamland is flanked by the slightly more challenging Bingin and Balangan and shares the same bay as the world-renowned Impossibles, Padang Padang and Uluwatu. Ulu in particular is synonymous with Bali surf thanks to its reputation as the Balinese proving ground. It is shallow, quick, hollow and heavy.

Although there are many, many more breaks on Bali (including Nusa Dua and Sri Lanka), the more intrepid surf traveller will usually want to leave the island and check out some of the other areas. In recent years, places such as the Mentawais have become accessible by boat, but initially most surfers still seem to head to the nearby islands of Nusa Lombongan and Lombok (and in particular, Desert Point). Both are peppered with amazing breaks and Lombok has a reputation as 'Bali before the fall'. Further east, the island of Sumbawa is home to the legendary Lakey Peak among others, and it is almost like visiting another country after the hectic Kuta.

Other islands with notable surf include Sumba, Sumatra and West Java. But aside from those already mentioned, the most famous wave in Indo is undoubtedly Grajagan, better known as G-Land. Discovered by Gerry Lopez and friends in the 1970s, and now run as private surf camps, G-land is described in the Stormrider Guide as a 'freight train left' and it is very definitely only for experienced surfers.

Profile: Rizal Tanjung

Rizal (pronounced 'Ree-zul') is associated with Indonesian surfing in the same way that Maradona is associated with Argentinian football. In a country with a surf culture that is growing exponentially, and in which young Balinese and Indonesian rippers are ripe for heroes they can worship, Rizal is largely credited with putting their country's scene on the map and proving that Indonesians can surf too. "I love to show them that," he said in an early interview. "It makes me feel proud to be who I am. It makes me feel lucky, thanks be to God."

Looking at his surfing, it's clear that Rizal has every reason to thank God. With his freakish combination of poise, grace, cojones and incredible natural talent, Rizal is one of the most graceful surfers you're ever going to see. His renown is such that, on the beaches of The Bukit, his name is spoken with a whispered reverence by locals and foreigners alike. On my first visit to Dreamland, and in the company of a new acquaintance, I watched Uluwatu fire in the distance. "Nobody takes off deeper than Rizal when it's like that," my companion said reverently. "Nobody."

Frontside power over an Indonesian left.

Tucked-in, backhand barrel ride.

So where did the young prodigy acquire such skills? Although it might appear that Rizal appeared fully-formed the moment he scored the cover of *Surfing* in 1995, in reality he served his apprenticeship the old-fashioned way: with application and determination. At the age of eight, his brother initially introduced him to the waves and taught him to stand, at Half Way break in Kuta. These were the formative years, during which Rizal sustained his first serious injury (a laceration to the head that scared him enough to quit for a year) and branched out to surf other breaks such as Bali Barrel and Padang Padang. It was also around this time that the important figure of Made Switra made an appearance in Rizal's life. Switra, a couple of years older than Tanjung, was also forcing his way onto the international scene and Rizal began to hang out with him and surf Bali Barrel more and more often. By the time he was 11, he was skilled enough to enter his first contest – the Japanese Indonesian Surfing Association Open. Rizal was awarded Best Performance, and on the back of this and a bit of early PR from his mum, he managed to get his first proper board (Rizal's mother told Australian board-shaper Paul Nicholls about her son; clearly impressed, Nicholls sorted the youngster out with a board). Until this point he'd been sharing with boards with friends. This marked a turning point.

By 1988, at the age of 12, Rizal had begun to tackle Uluwatu. Anybody who has seen this legendary break in full cry will appreciate just what a gnarly undertaking this is. By 1990, his skills had progressed to the point that he won the World Grommet Title, and now Rizal was at a crossroads: surf or school? Encouraged by his family, he quit school and set off on his first trip overseas, to Australia. Rizal's career seemed to be running in tandem with the fledgling Indonesian surf industry, which was experiencing a boom in the early 90s. For Rizal, it was a definite place of 'right place/right time', and by 1992, when companies such as Quiksilver opened their operation on the island, Rizal found himself in the middle of a sponsorship battle. He listened to the advice of friends and mentors, and made his choice. "Quiksilver came along and gave me a better deal. Made Kasim said I should go with them, and Made Switra was with them, so I went with Quiksilver too." It was a good choice, and Rizal turned pro in '94.

Grab the rail, get the front hand in the wall and hope…

For the next few years, Rizal lived the life of the modern travelling competitive surfer. He was Indo's highest ranker on the World Qualifying Series and scored wildcard invites to the G-Land Quicksilver Pro. But perhaps his biggest early triumph was winning the Dompu Open in Sumbawa against a high-class field. He took home $5,000 and the respect of the rest of the field. Soon after, he was back on the road, the highest-profile Indonesian to run the tour and stay on the road surfing for ten months a year. It wasn't long before he scored his biggest earliest career coup: that cover of *Surfer* with one of surfing's most iconic shots from the mid-90s: Rizal at Pipeline getting barrelled by what was the 'wave of the winter'. With these achievements, Rizal was promoting his country and its surf culture, slowly putting Indo on the map in a professional sense, and becoming synonymous with the scene. Interviewed in 1998, he gave some clue as to his motivations: "I'd like to concentrate on promoting Indonesian surfing. There're so many good spots and the potential to host heaps more events here than is now the case. Bringing more international events here is what's gonna help local surfers to get known and get surfing overseas."

A modern-day quiver of tube arrows.

Today Rizal is still charging hard. He's still the man at Padang Padang and Ulu's. If anything, the legend is growing on The Bukit. He's still in the videos, still scoring epic shots in the magazine, and, perhaps more importantly, still aware of his responsibility to the home scene. To this end, he opened a clothing shop (Electrohell) and club (Maximum Rock N Roll) in Kuta not long after the atrocity that rent the place apart in 2002. "It's gonna be the new place to hang out," he said at the time. "There is no more Sari club, and we needed something new and different. We made something like the CBGB [sic] in New York. We're the new generation and we care about our 'hood."

This willingness to put something back into the home country is something emerging scenes have in common all over the world, but it seems particularly strong in Indo. Strands of it can be seen throughout Rizal's surfing life: from his willingness to learn from a very early age, the way he was mentored first by his local bros and later by some of the bigger hotshots, and by the way he is superaware of the debt he feels he must repay to the scene that gave him so much. It's an attitude that seems to suffuse Indo surfing as a whole, and has the happy by-product of making Indo one of the friendliest places to surf in the world. As the book *Surfing Indonesia* puts it, "In Hawaii, you're an asshole until proven otherwise. In Bali, you're OK until you behave like an asshole." In this light, there's no better ambassador to be leading by example than Rizal Tanjung.

PICTURE CREDITS

The publishers would like to thanks the following sources for their kind permission to reproduce the pictures in this book. The page numbers for each of the photographs are listed below, giving the page on which they appear in the book. Any location indicator is as follows (c-centre, t-top, b-bottom, l-left, r-right)

2–3: Quiksilver/shine
6–7: Red Bull
8–9: Jackovitch/West
10: Quiksilver/shine
11: Red Bull
12–13: Quiksilver/shine
14–15: Surfer: Todd Morcom/ Sole Technology
16–17: (l) Quiksilver, (r) License plate: christianblack.com
18–19: (l) Sam Lamiroy/O'Neill (r) Scenic: christianblack.com
20–21: Surfer: Jake Boex/O'Neill

22–23: christianblack.com
24–25: Surfer: Gerry Lopez/Jeff Johnson
27: Surfer: Gerry Lopez/Zuma/Corbis
28–29: Sole Technology
30–31: Surfer: Keala Kennelly/Billabong
32–33: Surfer: Unknown/Quiksilver
34–35: Surfer: Kelly Slater/Quiksilver
36–37: (l) Surfer: Matt Manners/West (r) Surfer: unknown/Quiksilver
38–39: Quiksilver
40–41: (l) Surfer: Jackovitch/West (r) Surfer: Conan Hayes/Sole Technology
42–43: (l) Surfer: Cory Lopez/O'Neill (r) Surfer: Saxon Boucher/Hurley
44–45: Surfer: Lisa Anderson/ Quiksilver/Roxy
46–47: Surfer: Lisa Anderson/Roxy
48–49: Surfer: Kelly Slater/Quiksilver
50–51: Surfer: Kelly Slater/Quiksilver
52–53: Surfer: Conan Hayes/Sole Technology
54–55: (l) Billabong (r) Both shots: Surfer: Nathan Webster/West
56–57: Surfer: Keith Malloy/Sole Technology
58–59: Surfer: Conan Hayes/Sole Technology

60–61: (l) Quiksilver, (r) Quiksilver
62–63: Surfer: Occy/Billabong
64–65: Surfer: Occy/Reuters/Corbis
66–67: Surfer: Layne Beachley/Scott Needham/SNP5000.com
68–69: Surfer: Layne Beachley/Scott Needham/SNP5000.COM
70–71: Surfer: Layne Beachley/ © ASPWORLDTOUR/KAREN
72–73: Surfer: Sam Lamiroy/Red Bull
74–75: Surfer: Luke Stedman/Quiksilver
76–77: (l) Black and white: christianblack.com, (r) Quiksilver
78–79: (l) Black and white: John Issac, (r) Surfer: Gabe Davies/Stuart Norton
80–81: (l) Quiksilver, (r) John Isaac
82–83: Surfer: Luke Egan/Quiksilver
84–85: ACM
86–87: christianblack.com
88–89: (l) Surfer: Dan Waddell/West (r) Surfer: Flavio/Scott Needham/SNP5000.com
90–91: Surfer: Flavio/Scott Needham/SNP5000.com

92–93: Surfer: Grant Baker/ www.redbullbwa.com
94–95: Main: christianblack.com (r): Craig Peterson
96–97: Shark: christianblack.com, (r) www.redbullbwa.com
98–99: (l) Surfer: Dan Thorn/Red Bull, (r) Credit: Craig Peterson
100–101: Craig Peterson
102–103: Surfer: Stu Brass/ ACM
104–105: Quiksilver
106–107: Quiksilver
108–109: Both: Quiksilver
110–111(l) Quiksilver, (r) ACM shot
112: Quiksilver

Every effort has been made to acknowledge correctly and contact the source and/or copyright holder of each picture and Carlton Books Limited apologises for any unintentional errors or omissions that will be corrected in future editions of this book.